THANKSGIVING Cookbook

How to Make a Delicious Turkey Dinner

(Healthy Recipes to Celebrate Holidays)

Jack Wilkins

Published by Alex Howard

© Jack Wilkins

All Rights Reserved

Thanksgiving Cookbook: How to Make a Delicious Turkey Dinner (Healthy Recipes to Celebrate Holidays)

ISBN 978-1-989891-94-0

All rights reserved. No part of this guide may be reproduced in any form without permission in writing from the publisher except in the case of brief quotations embodied in critical articles or reviews.

Legal & Disclaimer

The information contained in this book is not designed to replace or take the place of any form of medicine or professional medical advice. The information in this book has been provided for educational and entertainment purposes only.

The information contained in this book has been compiled from sources deemed reliable, and it is accurate to the best of the Author's knowledge; however, the Author cannot guarantee its accuracy and validity and cannot be held liable for any errors or omissions. Changes are periodically made to this book. You must consult your doctor or get professional medical advice before using any of the suggested remedies, techniques, or information in this book.

Table of contents

Part 1 1
Introduction 2
Chapter One- Appetizers 3
Sausage-Cheese Balls 3
Bacon Roll Ups 3
Caraway Mini-puffs 5
Sweet Pepper Focaccia 6
Cocktail Meat Balls 7
Stuffed Jalapeno Peppers 8
Baked Buffalo Wings 9
Fried Pickles 10
Twice-Baked New Potatoes 11
Stuffed mushrooms 12
Chinese Chicken Wings 13
Pine Cone Cheese Balls 14
Savory cheese ball 15
Holiday appetizer Puffs 16
Spicy Deviled Eggs 17
Cheesy Christmas Trees 18
Sensational Seasonal Snack 19
Santa Fe Trail Mix 20
Chapter Two 21
Breakfast and Brunch 21

Pumpkin-Apple Muffins 21

Cinnamon Crumb Banana Muffins 23

Broccoli-Chicken Muffins 24

Jelly-Topped Peanut Butter Muffins 25

Yogurt Fruit Salad 26

Hamwiches 26

Pepperoni Pinwheels 27

Raisin Bran English Muffin Loaf 28

Lemon-Cream Loaf 29

Cranberry Nut Bread 30

Cinnamon Toast 32

Cheese Toasties 33

Christmas Pretzel Danish 34

Chapter 3: Main Dishes 36

Herb Roasted Rack of Lamb 36

Cranberry-Orange Game Hens 37

Prime Rib with Horseradish Cream Sauce 38

Horseradish Cream Sauce 38

Herb-Crusted Roast Beef 39

Sunshine-Glazed Ham 40

Ham Royale 41

Crown Roast with Cranberry-Pecan Stuffing 42

Cranberry-Pecan Stuffing 44

Pork Roast with Corn Bread & Oyster Stuffing 45

Simple Roast Duckling 46

Roast Turkey with Chestnut Stuffing 47
Cajun Deep-Fried Turkey 48
Turkey in a Bag 50
Turkey Gravy 51
Turkey Breast Stuffed with Wild Rice & Cranberries 52
Turkey in Cranberry Leek Sauce 52
Sweet Potato Stuffing 53
Slow-Cooker Turkey 54
Stuffing Recipes 55
Bread Stuffing with Onions and Celery 55
Oyster Stuffing 56
Sausage and Bread Stuffing 56
Chapter 4: Side Dishes 57
Green Beans with Almonds 57
Tangerine Sweet Potatoes 57
Twice Baked Sweet Potatoes 58
Butterbeans with Bacon and Green Onions 59
Mediterranean Caramelized Onions 60
Sautéed Portobello Mushrooms 61
Green Beans, Walnut and Feta Salad 61
Tangy Mixed Vegetables 62
Wild Rice with Apricots and Cranberries 63
Golden Apples and Yams 64
Green Beans with Blue Cheese 65
Marinated Brussels Sprouts 66

Broccoli with Parmesan Sauce 66

Brussels Sprouts with Pecans 68

Steamed Zucchini with Green Onions 69

Cheesy Mashed Potatoes with Gouda 69

Garlic Mashed Potatoes 70

Au Gratin Potatoes 71

Creamed Corn 72

Parmesan Asparagus 72

Thai Green Bean Casserole 73

Cauliflower with Peas and Mushrooms 74

Sautéed Cherry Tomatoes with Garlic and Basil 75

Chapter 5: Holiday Pies 75

Easy Pie Crust 76

Classic Pecan Pie 76

Almond Amaretto Pie 77

Butterscotch Pecan Pie 78

Bourbon Pecan Pie 78

Pumpkin Cheese-Swirl Pie 79

Apple Brandy Praline Pie 80

Praline Topping 81

Blueberry Pie 81

Pumpkin Pie 82

Sweet Potato Pie 83

Caramel Crunch Cheesecake 83

Chocolate Raspberry Cheesecake 85

Brownie Bottom Cheesecake 85

Pumpkin Marble Cheese Cake 86

Chapter 6: Bars and Cookies 87

Holiday Cheese Cake Bars 88

Snowmen Cookies 88

Shortbread cookies 89

Frosted Pumpkin Squares 90

Creamy Lemon Bars 91

Sugar Cookies 92

Pecan Pie Bars 92

Bar Cookie Crust 93

Almond Toffee Triangles 93

Chocolate Chip Walnut Bars 94

Cranberry Walnut Bars 95

Cherry Nut Thumbprints 96

Chocolate Peppermint Cookies 96

Granola Meringue Cookies 97

Fudgy Mint Brownies 98

Persimmon cookies 99

Chapter 7: Breads and Rolls 101

Pandoro 101

"Sponge" 102

Parmesan Bread Twists 103

French Honey-Spice Bread 104

Country Oatmeal Bread 105

Pumpernickel Brie Wreath 106
Easy Dinner Rolls 107
Almond-Anise Biscotti 109
Cinnamon Twists 110
Orange-Cranberry Bread 111
Chapter 8: Holiday Desserts and Cakes 114
Cantaloupe-Champagne Sorbet 114
Refreshing Lime Sherbet 114
Frozen Pumpkin Dessert 115
Tropical Frozen Yogurt 116
Mango-Pineapple Sorbet 117
Pumpkin Mousse 117
Sweet Roll Pudding 118
Steamed Holiday Pudding 119
Flamed Plum Pudding 120
Belgian Mocha Cake 122
Mocha Frosting 124
Black Walnut Cake 124
Cream Cheese Frosting 126
Fig Preserve Cake 126
Buttermilk Glaze 128
Italian Cream Cake 128
Nutty Cream Cheese Frosting 130
Pumpkin-Pecan Tube Cake 130
Brandied Fruit Cake 131

Chapter 9: Dips, Sauces and Spreads 133

Hot Crab Dip 133

Curry Onion Dip 133

Blue Cheese Dip 134

Antipasto Dip 135

Nacho Dip.. 136

Sweet and Spicy Mustard Dip 137

Quick Jalapeño Pepper Jelly 137

Southwestern Salsa with Black Beans and Corn............................. 138

Cranberry Chutney 138

Raspberry Vinaigrette 139

Cranberry Maple Butter 140

Dutch-Apple Butter 141

Breakfast Prune Butter 141

Spiced Plum Butter 142

Homemade Apple Sauce 143

Banana Sundae Sauce 144

Fresh Cranberry Sauce 144

Raisin Sauce.. 145

Honey-Lemon Mustard Sauce 146

Pineapple Rum Sauce.. 146

Chapter 10: Punches and Drinks 147

Autumn Harvest Punch 147

Berry-Colada Punch 148

Golden Fruit Punch 148

Fruit Juice Punch 149

Sunset Punch 150

Cranberry Punch 150

Christmas Punch 151

Mocha Coffee 151

White Russian Coffee 152

Irish Coffee Nog 152

Mexican Mocha 153

Mexican Rice Drink (Horchata) 154

Milk Punch 155

Bug Juice 155

Chapter 11: Leftover Ham and Turkey Recipes 156

Cheesy Ham and Potato Casserole 156

Ham and Vegetable Quiche 157

Ham Salad with Tortillas 158

Turkey and Dressing Pie 159

Turkey al La King 160

Conclusion 161

Part 2 162

Introduction 163

Slow Cooker Corn Chowder 164

2. Moist & Tender Turkey Breast 165

3. Gingerbread Pudding Cake 165

4. Green Bean Casserole 167

5. Hot Mulled Ginger-Spiced Cider 167

6. Grandma Dean's Chicken and Dressing 169
7. Steamed Brown Bread with Currants and Walnuts 169
8. Butternut Squash Soup.. 171
9. Mashed Potatoes 172
10. Cranberry-Orange Mulled Wine.. 173
11. Balsamic Brussels Sprouts... 175
12. Cranberry Sauce.. 176
13. Pecan Pie 177
14. Caramel Apple Crumble 178
15. Chocolate Cake 179
16. Sage and Sausage Stuffing Recipe... 180
17. Quinoa-Stuffed Peppers 182
18. Garlic Mashed Potatoes 183
19. Pumpkin Cobbler.. 184
20. Apple Barbecue Pulled Turkey Sandwiches........................ 185
21. Sweet Potato Turkey Shepherds Pie....................................... 186

Part 1

Introduction

Create a memorable holiday season with Thanksgiving and Christmas Recipes. For impressive holiday meals, breads desserts and pies: Turkey still reigns supreme as an time honored celebration, but for new ideas serve it with some new trendy side dishes, choose from a wide array of side dishes, desserts, dips or sauces cookies to baked breads.

Get Comfortable with the meal you have chosen.

Because the rest of the meal follows naturally after you've picked a main course, keep appetizers and brunch items light; your family and guests have a special meal being prepared. Thanksgiving and Christmas Recipes has a great collection of new and traditional side dishes, desserts and pies; these can be prepared a few days ahead or frozen and thawed the night before. Enjoy: Have a great holiday season:

Chapter One- Appetizers

Sausage-Cheese Balls

3 cups original Bisquick baking mix
1 pound uncooked bulk sausage
4 cups shredded cheddar cheese
½ cup grated parmesan cheese
½ cup milk
½ teaspoon dried rosemary, crumbled
1½ teaspoons chopped fresh parsley or ½ teaspoon dried parsley flakes

Directions

1. Preheat oven to 350 degrees F. Lightly grease jelly roll pan. 15½ x 10 x 1-inch
2. Blend all ingredients until well mixed. Shape into 1-inch balls.
3. Bake 20 to 25 minutes or until brown. Immediately remove from pan Serve warm.
Makes about 8 dozen appetizers

-

Bacon Roll Ups

¼ cup soy sauce
2 tablespoons white sugar
2 (5 oz.) cans water chestnuts, drained
10 slices bacon, cut in half

Directions

1. Preheat oven to 350 degrees F. Line shallow baking pan with foil.
2. Combine soy sauce and sugar. Stir in water chestnuts. Marinate chestnuts overnight.
2. Wrap bacon slice around each chestnut. Fasten with a wooden toothpick. Place on a rack in shallow prepared baking pan.
3. Bake at 350 degrees F for 35-45 minutes or until bacon is crispy. Serve hot.

Males 20 Appetizers

Note: Bacon may be cut into third of you prefer.

Caraway Mini-puffs

1 cup water
½ cup margarine or butter
1 cup self-rising flour
1 teaspoon caraway seeds
4 eggs

Directions

Preheat oven to 400 degrees F In a 2-quart sauce pan heat water and margarine to a rolling boil. Stir in flour and caraway seeds; reduce heat to low. Cook about 1 minute, stirring vigorously, until mixture forms a ball; remove from heat.
Beat in eggs, all at the same time; continue beating until smooth. Drop dough by rounded teaspoons 2-inches apart on ungreased cookie sheet.
Bake 25 to 30 minutes or until puffed and golden. Cool on wire rack. Store in plastic food storage bags or an airtight container at room temperature up to 2 days.
Makes 6 dozen puffs

Sweet Pepper Focaccia

Keep focaccia in the freezer, for quick and tasty meals or appetizers, just top and serve

1 focaccia or Italian bread shell (12-in in diameter)
½ cup finely shredded pizza blend cheese (mozzarella and cheddar)
1 small red or green bell pepper, coarsely chopped
2 roma (plum) tomatoes, chopped
2 Tablespoons Italian dressing
2 Tablespoons grated Parmesan cheese
Fresh basil or oregano leaves, shredded, if desired

Directions

1. Preheat oven to 400 degrees F. Place focaccia on ungreased cookie sheet. Sprinkle evenly with pizza cheese blend. Top with bell pepper and tomatoes. Drizzle with dressing.
2. Bake about 10 minutes or until edge of focaccia is golden brown. Sprinkle with parmesan cheese and basil. Cut into 24 wedges
Makes 12 servings

Cocktail Meat Balls

Great Recipe to make ahead

1 envelope Lipton Recipe Secrets onion, onion mushroom or beefy onion soup mix
1 pound ground beef
½ cup plain dry bread crumbs
¼ cup dry red wine or water
2 eggs, slightly beaten

Directions

1. Preheat oven to 375 degrees F.
2. In medium bowl, combine all ingredients; shape into 1-inch meat balls.
3. In a shallow baking pan, arrange meatballs and bake 18 minutes or until done. Serve, if desired, with assorted mustards or tomato sauce.

Makes about 4 dozen meatballs

Stuffed Jalapeno Peppers

12 ounces cream cheese, softened
8 ounce package shredded Cheddar cheese
1 tablespoon bacon bits
12 ounces jalapeno peppers, seeded and halved
1 cup milk
1 cup all-purpose flour
1 cup dry bread crumbs
Oil for frying

Directions

1. Blanch the peppers in almost boiling water for 2 minutes. Then let them cool.
2. In a medium bowl, mix the cream cheese, Cheddar cheese and bacon bits. Spoon this mixture into the jalapeno pepper halves.
3. Put the milk and flour into two separate small bowls. Dip the stuffed jalapenos first into the milk then into the flour, making sure they are well coated with each. Allow the coated jalapenos to dry for about 10 minutes.
4. Dip the jalapenos in milk again and roll them through the breadcrumbs. Allow them to dry, and then repeat to ensure the entire surface of the jalapeno is coated.
5. In a medium skillet, heat the oil to 365 degrees F. Deep fry the coated jalapenos 2 to 3 minutes each, until golden brown. Remove and drain on paper towels.

Baked Buffalo Wings

4 pounds chicken wings
3 Tablespoons cooking oil
4 cloves garlic, chopped
1 ¾ teaspoons salt
1 ½ teaspoons cayenne
2/3 cup mayonnaise
1/3 cup sour cream
¼ pound blue cheese, crumbled (about 1 cup)
 2 scallions including green tops, chopped
5 teaspoons vinegar
¼ teaspoon fresh-ground black pepper
¼ cup ketchup
1 Tablespoon Tabasco sauce

Directions

1. Preheat the oven to 425°. In a large bowl, combine the wings, oil, garlic, 1 ½ teaspoons of the salt, and the cayenne. Arrange the wings in a single layer on two large baking sheets. Bake 30 to 35 minutes or until just done..

2. **For Blue Cheese Dressing**. In a medium glass or stainless-steel bowl, combine the mayonnaise, sour cream, blue cheese, scallions, 1 teaspoon of the vinegar, the remaining ¼ teaspoon salt, and the black pepper.

3. In a large bowl, combine the ketchup, the remaining 4 teaspoons vinegar, and Tabasco sauce. Add the wings and toss to coat. Serve with the blue-cheese dressing.

Serve wings with. Corn on the cob would go nicely. Roasted potato wedges are a good alternative and can be cooked with the wings.

Fried Pickles

2 cups whole wheat flour
1 cup all-purpose flour
2 teaspoons salt
1 teaspoon paprika
¼ teaspoon cayenne pepper
1 (11 oz) jar hamburger dill pickle slices
2 cups buttermilk
Oil for frying

Directions

1. Preheat 8 cups of vegetable oil to 350 degrees F in a large pot or deep fryer. Drain dill pickles in a colander and then place into a medium sized bowl with the 2 cups of buttermilk. Place all dry ingredients into a bowl and mix well.
2. Take about a handful of the pickles out of the buttermilk and coat with the seasoned flour. Shake off excess flour, and place battered pickles into hot grease. Fry pickles in small batches, as too many pickles into the hot grease or the pickles won't fry up crisp. Fry pickle slices until golden brown. Continue cooking pickles until all are done.
3. Drain on paper towels. Be careful fried pickles as they retain their heat for quite some time.

Note: I have found Refrigerator pickles work best. And seem to hold the batter better.

Twice-Baked New Potatoes

1½ pounds small red potatoes
2 to 3 Tablespoons vegetable oil
1 cup shredded Monterey jack cheese
½ cup sour cream
1 (3oz.) pkg cream cheese, softened
1/3 cup Green onions, minced
1 teaspoon dried basil
1 garlic clove, minced
½ teaspoon salt
½ teaspoon pepper
½ pound sliced bacon, cooked and crumbled

Directions

1. Preheat oven to 400 degrees F. Pearce potatoes; rub skins with oil. Place in a baking pan. Bake; uncovered for about 50 minutes or until tender. Allow to cool.
2. In a mixing bowl, combine Monterey jack cheese, sour cream, cream cheese, green onion, basil, garlic, salt and pepper.
3. Cut potatoes in half; carefully scoop out the pulp, leaving a thin shell. Add pulp to the cheese mixture and mash; stir in bacon. Stuff the potato shells. Broil for 7 to 8 minutes or until heated through
Makes about 2 dozen

Stuffed mushrooms

24 large mushrooms (about 1 pound) cleaned
½ pound ground turkey
1 garlic clove, minced
¼ cup fine bread crumbs
¼ cup thinly sliced green onions
3 tablespoons reduced-sodium soy sauce (divided)
1 egg white lightly beaten
1 teaspoon minced ginger
¼ teaspoon red pepper flakes (optional)

Directions

1. Remove stems from mushrooms; finely chop enough stems to make 1 cup. Cook turkey with the chopped mushroom stems and garlic in medium skillet over medium high heat until turkey is no longer pink, stirring to separate turkey. Spoon off any fat and discard. Stir in bread crumbs, green onions, 2 tablespoons soy sauce, egg white, ginger and pepper flakes if desired; mix well.
2. Preheat broiler; line broiler pan with foil. Brush mushrooms caps lightly on all sides with remaining 1 tablespoon soy sauce; spoon about 2 teaspoons stuffing into each mushroom cap. Place stuffed mushrooms caps on rack of prepared pan Broil 4-5 inches from heat; cook for 5-6 minutes or until hot.

Chinese Chicken Wings

2 cups soy sauce
2 cups brown sugar
2 tablespoons garlic powder
4 pounds chicken wings split and tips discarded

Directions

1. Stir the soy sauce, brown sugar, and garlic powder together in a saucepan over medium heat; cook and stir until the sugar melts completely. Remove from heat and allow cooling.
2. Place the chicken wings in a large bowl. Pour the soy sauce mixture over the wings and toss to coat evenly. Cover the bowl with plastic wrap. Allow chicken to marinate in refrigerator overnight or at least 8 hours.
3. Preheat an oven to 350 degrees F.
Pour the chicken wings and marinade into a 9x13-inch baking dish. Cover the baking dish with aluminum foil.
4. Bake about 45 minutes. Remove aluminum and continue baking uncovered for another 15 minutes. Serve hot.

Pine Cone Cheese Balls

2 cups shredded Swiss cheese
½ cup butter
3 Tablespoons milk
2 Tablespoons dry sherry or milk
1/8 teaspoon ground red pepper
1 cup finely chopped blanched almonds
¾ cup sliced almonds
½ cup whole almonds
Rosemary
Crackers

Directions
1. Beat cheese, butter, milk, sherry, and red pepper in a medium bowl until smooth; stir in chopped almonds.
2. Divide mixture into 3 equal portions; shape each into tapered ovals to resemble pine cones. Insert slivered, sliced and whole almonds into the cones. Cover and refrigerate 2 to 3 hours or until firm.
3. Arrange pine cones on wooden cheese board or serving platter. Garnish with rosemary. Serve with crackers
Makes 12 to 16 appetizer servings

Savory cheese ball

1 (8-oz) pkg cream cheese, softened
1 (8-oz) package sharp Cheddar cheese
¾ cup crumbled blue cheese
¼ cup chopped green onions
2 Tablespoons milk
1 teaspoon Worcestershire sauce
Finely chopped walnuts or pecans

Directions

1. Mix cheeses, green onions, milk and Worcestershire sauce until well blended. Refrigerate 1 to 2 hours.
2. Shape into a ball; roll in chopped walnuts. Serve with apple slices or crackers.
Makes 2-2/3 cups

Holiday appetizer Puffs

1 sheet frozen puff pastry, thawed (half 17 ½ -oz package)
2 Tablespoons olive oil or vegetable oil
Toppings: Parmesan cheese, sesame seeds, poppy seeds, dried dill weed, dried basil leaves, paprika, stuffed green olive slices

Directions

1. Preheat oven to 425 degrees F. Roll pastry on lightly floured surface to 13-inch square. Cut into shapes with cookie cutters (simple-shaped cutters work best, like Christmas trees bells and stars etc). Place on ungreased baking sheet.
2. Brush cut-outs lightly with oil. Decorate with desired toppings.
3. Bake 6 to 8 minutes or until golden, serve warm or room temperature,
Makes 18 appetizers

Spicy Deviled Eggs

1 dozen large eggs, hard-cooked and peeled
6 tablespoons mayonnaise
3 Tbsp. pickled sliced jalapeño peppers, minced
1 Tablespoon mustard
1/2 teaspoon cumin
1/8 teaspoon salt
Garnish: chopped fresh cilantro

Directions

Cut eggs in half lengthwise and carefully remove yolks. Mash yolks; stir in mayonnaise and next 4 ingredients. Spoon or pipe; egg yolk mixture into egg white halves. Cover and chill at least 1 hour or until ready to serve. Garnish, if desired.
Makes 24 deviled eggs
Note: Fresh eggs are harder to peel: Buy eggs and refrigerate 7 to 10 days for easy peeling.

Cheesy Christmas Trees

½ cup mayonnaise
1 Tablespoon dry ranch-style salad dressing
1 cup shredded cheddar cheese
¼ cup grated parmesan cheese
12 slices firm white bread
¼ cup red pepper strips
¼ cup green bell pepper strips

Directions

1. Preheat broiler: Combine mayonnaise and salad dressing mix in a medium bowl. Add cheeses; mix well.
2. Cut bread slices into Christmas tree shapes using large cookie cutter. Spread each tree with about 1 Tablespoon mayo mixture. Decorate with red and green bell pepper strips. Place on baking sheet.
3. Broil 4 inches from heat 2 to 3 minutes or until bubbling. Serve warm.
Makes 12 appetizers

Sensational Seasonal Snack

2 cups oatmeal cereal squares
12 cups corn cereal squares
2 cups mini pretzels
1 cup whole almonds
¼ cup butter
1/3 cup frozen orange juice concentrate, thawed
3 Tablespoon packed brown sugar
1 teaspoon ground cinnamon
¾ teaspoon ground ginger
¼ teaspoon ground nutmeg
2/3 cup dried cranberries

Directions

1. Preheat oven to 250 degrees F. Spray 13x9-inch baking pan with nonstick cooking spray.
2. Combine cereal squares, pretzels and almonds in a large bowl, set aside.
3. Melt butter in medium microwave bowl on HIGH 45 to 60 seconds, Stir in orange juice concentrate, brown sugar, cinnamon, ginger and nutmeg until well blended, Pour over cereal mixture; stir well to coat. Place in prepared pan and spread to one layer.
4. Bake 50 minutes, stirring every 10 minutes. Stir in cranberries. Let cool in pan on wire rack, leaving uncovered until mixture is crisp. Store in airtight container or resealable plastic storage bag.
Makes 8 Cups

Santa Fe Trail Mix

1 ½ cups pecans halves
1 cup cashews
¾ cup roasted shelled pistachio nuts
½ cup pine nuts
1/3 cup roasted sunflower seeds
3 Tablespoons butter
2 ½ teaspoons ground cumin
¼ teaspoon garlic powder
¼ cup plus 1 Tbsp. chili sauce
1 chipotle Chile in adobo sauce, about 3-inch long
1 Tablespoon frozen orange juice concentrate, thawed
Cooking spray
1 Tablespoon dried cilantro, divided

Directions

1. Preheat oven to 300 degrees F. Line 14x11-inch baking sheet with foil, set aside
2. Combine pecans, cashews, pistachios, pine nuts and sunflower seeds in a large bowl.
3. Combine butter, cumin and garlic powder in small microwavable bowl. Microwave on High 45 to 50 seconds or until butter is melted and foamy; stir to blend.
4. Place butter mixture, chili sauce, chipotle Chile and orange juice concentrate in food processor or blender; process until smooth. Pour sauce over nut mixture; stir to evenly coat. Spread mixture in single layer on prepared baking sheet.
5. Bake about 1 hour, stirring every 10 minutes. Remove from oven and spray mixture evenly with cooking spray. Sprinkle 1 ½ teaspoons cilantro over mixture. Stir mixture with spatula and repeat with additional cooking spray and remaining cilantro. Set baking sheet on wire rack to cool. Leave uncovered at least 1

hour before storing in airtight container or resealable plastic bag.

Chapter Two

Breakfast and Brunch

Thanksgiving and Christmas; here is a collection of time saving recipes that can be made ahead and frozen or refrigerated until ready to serve; on the busy morning also helps keep kids busy and safe from the kitchen.

Pumpkin-Apple Muffins

Hot baked apples are the perfect side dish with these hearty brunch muffins

1 2/3 cups all-purpose flour
1 teaspoon baking powder
½ teaspoon baking soda
¼ teaspoon salt
1 Tablespoon pumpkin pie spice
1 cup sugar
1 cup canned pumpkin
½ cup butter or margarine, melted
2 large eggs, lightly beaten
1 Granny smith apple, peeled and finely chopped
3 Tablespoons sugar
1 teaspoon pumpkin pie spice

Directions

1. Preheat oven to 350 degrees F: Grease or line with paper liners two 12 cup muffin pans.
2. In a large bowl, combine first 6 ingredients; make a well in center of mixture.
3. Combine pumpkin, butter and eggs; add to dry ingredients, stirring just until moistened. Fold in chopped apple, and spoon into muffin pans, filling two-thirds full Combine 3 Tablespoons sugar and 1 teaspoon pumpkin pie spice; sprinkle evenly over muffins.
4. Bake in preheated oven for 20 minutes. Remove from pan immediately, cool on wire racks.
Makes 2 dozen

Cinnamon Crumb Banana Muffins

1 ¾ cups plus 1 tablespoon all-purpose flour
1 ¼ teaspoons baking soda
1 ¼ teaspoons baking powder
½ teaspoon salt
3 or 4 bananas, mashed
¾ cup and 2 tablespoons and 1 teaspoon white sugar
1 large egg, lightly beaten
1/3 cup butter, melted
1 teaspoon vanilla
1/3 cup plus 1Tablespoon packed brown sugar
3 Tablespoons all-purpose flour
¾ teaspoon ground cinnamon
½ teaspoon nutmeg
1 Tablespoon cold butter

Directions

1. Preheat oven to 375 degrees F. Lightly grease 12 muffin cups, or line with papers or foil liners.
2. In a large bowl, mix together 1 ¾ cups flour, baking soda, baking powder and salt. In another bowl, beat together bananas, sugar, egg, vanilla and melted butter. Stir the banana mixture into the flour mixture just until moistened. Spoon batter into prepared muffin cups.
3. In a small bowl, mix together brown sugar, 3 tablespoons flour and cinnamon and nutmeg. Cut in 1 tablespoon butter until mixture resembles coarse cornmeal: Sprinkle topping over muffins.
4. Bake in preheated oven for 18 to 20 minutes, until a toothpick inserted into center of a muffin comes out clean.

Broccoli-Chicken Muffins

Also a great left-over Turkey recipe.

2 cups biscuit and baking mix
1/3 cup grated parmesan cheese
½ teaspoon black pepper
¼ teaspoon salt
¼ teaspoon garlic powder
1 large egg, lightly beaten
1 cup buttermilk
2 Tablespoons vegetable oil
1 cup chopped cooked broccoli
1 cup chopped cooked chicken

Directions

1. In a large bowl combine first 5 ingredients, make a well in the center of mixture.
2. Combine egg, buttermilk and oil; add to dry ingredients, stirring just until moistened. Stir in broccoli and chicken. Spoon into muffin pan, filling to the top
3. Bake at 425 degrees F. for 20 to 22 minutes. Remove from pan immediately. Cool on wire rack.
Makes 12 muffins

Jelly-Topped Peanut Butter Muffins

These muffins make a quick brunch or snack for even the finicky eaters.

1½ cups all-purpose flour
2 teaspoons baking powder
½ teaspoon salt
½ cup cornmeal
3 Tablespoons sugar
¾ cup chunky peanut butter
2 Tablespoons honey
2 large eggs
1 cup milk
¼ cup grape jelly or flavor of your choice

Directions

1. In a large bowl, combine first 5 ingredients; make a well in the cents of mixture.
2. Combine peanut butter and honey, stir well; add eggs and milk, stirring until blended. Add to dry ingredients; stirring until just moistened.
3. Spoon batter into greased; 12 cup muffin pan; filling three-fourths full. Spoon 1 teaspoon jelly in the center of each
4. Bake at 375 degrees F. for 20 minutes or until golden. Remove from pans immediately, cool on wire racks, Serve warm with additional jelly, if desired.
Makes 12 muffins

Yogurt Fruit Salad

1 (8-oz) can pineapple chucks, drained
1 (11-oz) can mandarin oranges, drained
1 cup miniature marshmallows
1 (8-oz) container vanilla yogurt

Directions

Combine all ingredients; tossing gently to coat; cover and chill.
Makes 4 Servings

Hamwiches

1 (8-oz) can refrigerator crescent rolls
1 Tablespoon mayonnaise
1 teaspoon prepared mustard
1 cup finely chopped ham
½ cup (2-oz) shredded Swiss cheese

Directions

1. Unroll dough, and separate into 4 rectangles; press seams to seal.
2. Combine mayo and mustard; spread over rectangles, leaving a ½ - inch border. Sprinkle ham and cheese evenly over each rectangle; moisten edges with water. Fold dough over, and pinch edges to seal
3. Bake at 375 degrees F: for 10 minutes or until Hamwiches are puffed and golden.
Makes 4 Servings

Note: Baked Hamwiches can be stored in an airtight container in the refrigerator for up to 1 week.

Pepperoni Pinwheels

1 (10-oz) can refrigerated pizza crust
1 cup (4-oz) shredded mozzarella cheese
½ (3.5-oz) pkg. sliced pepperoni, chopped
½ cup spaghetti sauce

Directions

1. Unroll refrigerated pizza crust on a cutting board; sprinkle with cheese and pepperoni. Roll up, starting with long side; moisten edges with water, and pinch edges to seal.
2. Place in freezer for 20 minutes to make cutting easier. Cut into 2-inch slices and place 1 inch apart in a lightly greased 15x10x1-inch jellyroll pan; flatten slightly.
3. Bake at 400 degrees F: for 15 to 20 minutes; serve with warm spaghetti sauce, if desired. My 5 year-old grandson like's ranch dressing
Makes 8 Servings

Note: Baked Pinwheels can be stored in an airtight container in the refrigerator for up to 1 week, or may be frozen and slices and baked when you are ready. As in step 2

Raisin Bran English Muffin Loaf

2 cups whole wheat flour
2 packages dry yeast
¾ teaspoon salt
¼ teaspoon baking powder
2 cups milk
½ cup water
1 Tablespoon honey
1 cup unprocessed wheat bran
1/3 cup raisins, chopped
2 ½ cups all-purpose flour
Vegetable cooking spray
2 Tablespoons cornmeal, divided

Directions

1. Combine whole wheat flour, yeast, salt and baking powder; stir well. In a small saucepan, combine milk, water and honey; cook over medium heat until very warm (120 to 130 degrees F.)
2. Gradually add milk mixture to flour mixture, beating with an electric mixer at medium speed for about 3 minutes. Gradually stir in bran, raisins and enough all-purpose flour to make stiff dough.
3. Coat two 8 ½ x 4 ½ x 3-inch loaf pans with cooking spray; sprinkle each pan with 2 teaspoons cornmeal. Spoon batter evenly into pans; cover and let rise in a warm place (85 degrees), 30 to 45 minutes or until doubled in size. Bake at 400 degrees F. Bake for 25 minutes or until toothpick inserted in the center comes out clean. Remove from pans immediately, and let cool on wire racks.
Makes 32 Servings

Lemon-Cream Loaf

This recipe is our favorite recipe; try adding 1 cup of blueberries and 1 Tablespoon of grated lemon peel to the batter and omit the nuts.

1 (8-oz) pkg cream cheese, softened
½ cup butter or margarine, softened
1 ¼ cup sugar
2 eggs
2 ¼ cups all-purpose flour
1 Tablespoon baking powder
½ teaspoon salt
¾ cup milk or buttermilk
2/3 cup chopped pecans
1 teaspoon grated lemon rind
2 to 3 Tablespoons lemon juice
1/3 cup sifted powdered sugar

Directions

1. Preheat oven to 350 degrees F. Grease and lightly floured two 8 ½ x 4 ½ x3 loaf pans.
2. Combine cream cheese and butter, blend well. Gradually add sugar; beating until light and fluffy. Add eggs, one at a time, beating mixture well after each addition.
3. Combine flour, baking powder and salt; add to creamed mixture alternately with milk, beginning and ending with flour mixture. Mix well after each addition. Stir in pecans
4. Pour batter in prepared pans. Bake for 45 minutes or until toothpick inserted comes out clean. Combine lemon rind,

Lemon juice and powdered sugar, mixing until smooth; pour over hot loaves. Cool in pans for 10 minutes; transfer to wire racks to cool completely.
Makes 2 loaves

Cranberry Nut Bread

This festive, fruity quick bread has become a favorite Thanksgiving and Christmas gift. The cranberries give the bread a juicy, tart bite that offsets the sweet, cakey crumb. This recipe can be easily adapted to make muffins as well as many other flavored loaves

1 Tablespoon oil, to grease pan
1¾ unbleached flour plus extra to dust pan
1 ½ teaspoons baking powder
½ teaspoons baking soda
½ teaspoon salt
½ cup (60g) pecans, coarsely chopped
1 egg, beaten
¼ cup milk
2/3 cup sugar
4 Tablespoons unsalted butter, melted
1 ½ cups (175g) cranberries

Directions

1. Grease a 9in x 5in x 3in (22x12x7cm) loaf pan with oil. Dust generously with flour.
Preheat oven to 350 degrees F. (180 C)
2. Sift the flour, baking powder, baking soda, and salt in a large bowl. Stir in the pecans and make a well in the center. Place the remaining ingredients in a separate bowl and mix until thoroughly combined.

3. Pour the mixture and the cranberries into the well. Use a spatula to gently fold all ingredients together to form a wet batter (Over-mixing can result in a heavy batter)

4. Spoon the batter into the prepared loaf pan. Bake in the preheated oven for 1 hour, until golden and well-risen. The bread is ready when the edges shrink from the sides of the pan, and tooth pick inserted into the center comes out clean.

5. Keep the bread in the pan and let stand, about 10 minutes. Carefully run a knife around the edges and turn out. Cool on wire rack.

Cinnamon Toast

This is an old fashioned snack that is warming and comforting on a cold day. Cinnamon toast is perfect with a spicy hot chocolate drink or a few slices of fresh fruit.
Prep: 2 minutes: Cooking: 2-3 minutes

3 oz. butter, softened
2 teaspoons ground cinnamon
2 tablespoon superfine sugar, plus extra to serve
4 slices bread
Prepared fresh fruit such as peaches, plumbs, nectarines or mangos (optional)

Directions

Place the softened butter in a bowl. Beat with a spoon until soft and creamy, mix in the ground cinnamon and most of the sugar. Toast the bread. Spread with butter and sprinkle with a little remaining sugar. Serve immediately, with fresh fruit, if desired

Cheese Toasties

Always a hit with small children, because of the way the egg and cheese mixture puffs up during baking; this is a nutritious and easy breakfast or snack that everyone will enjoy. Even a picky 5 year old will love this recipe

Prep: 3-4 minutes Cooking 10-15 minutes

2 eggs
8 oz. (1½ -2 cups) cheddar cheese, grated
1 teaspoon spicy brown mustard
4 slices bread, buttered
2-4 halved tomatoes (optional)
Ground black pepper
Watercress or fresh parsley (optional)

Directions

1. Preheat oven to 450 degrees F. (230C) Whisk the eggs lightly and stir in grated cheese, mustard and pepper.
2. Lay the buttered bread buttered side down in a shallow baking dish.
3. Divide the cheese mixture among the slices of bread, spreading evenly.
4. Bake for 10-15 minutes or until well risen and golden brown. Adding the halved tomatoes for a few minutes, if desired Serve immediately with sprigs of watercress or parsley, if desired

Christmas Pretzel Danish

½ cup warm milk
1 Tablespoon sugar
1 (.25 ounce); envelope active dry yeast
1 cup heavy cream
3 ½ cups all-purpose flour
1/4 cup sugar
1 teaspoon salt
1 teaspoon ground cardamom
½ cup butter
1 (8 ounce) can almond paste
½ cup crushed sliced almonds
½ cup sugar
1 teaspoon ground cinnamon
1 teaspoon almond extract
½ cup white sugar
1 egg white, beaten
½ cup sliced almonds

Directions

1. In a small bowl, blend together the milk and sugar. Sprinkle the yeast over the top and let stand for 10 minutes to dissolve. Stir in cream.
2. In a separate bowl, mix together the flour, sugar, salt and cardamom. Cut in the butter using a pastry blender or pinching with your fingers until it is a course bread crumb texture. Stir in the yeast mixture until well blended. Pat into a ball, flatten slightly, and then wrap in plastic wrap. Refrigerate for 12 to 24 hours.
3. **To make the filling**, with an electric mixer, blend the almond paste, almonds, sugar, cinnamon and almond extract until evenly blended. It may be crumbly.

4. Roll the chilled dough out into a 2 inch wide and 24 inch long rectangle. Spread the filling to within 2 inches of the sides and roll up into a tube. Cover surface with sugar, and roll the tube of dough in the sugar to coat thoroughly. Roll and stretch the dough out to form a long rope about 40 inches long. Place on a parchment lined baking sheet and shape into a pretzel shape.
5. Brush the top of the pretzel with egg white and sprinkle with almonds. Cover loosely with a towel and let rise for 45 minutes.
6. Meanwhile: Preheat the oven to 375 degrees F. Bake the pretzel in the preheated oven until golden brown, 25 to 30 minutes. Cut into slices to serve.

Chapter 3: Main Dishes

Herb Roasted Rack of Lamb

½ cup mango chutney, chopped
2 to 3 garlic cloves, minced
2 whole racks (6 ribs each) lamb loin chops
1 cup fresh French or Italian bread crumbs
1 Tablespoon chopped fresh thyme or 1 teaspoon dried thyme
1 Tablespoon chopped fresh rosemary or 1 teaspoon dried Rosemary
1 Tablespoon chopped fresh oregano or 1 teaspoon dried oregano

Directions

1. Preheat oven to 400 degrees F. In a small bowl, combine chutney and garlic; spread evenly over meaty side of lamb with a thin spatula... Combine remaining ingredients in a small bowl; pat crumb mixture evenly over chutney mixture.
2. Place lamb racks, crumb side up, on rack in shallow roasting pan. Roast in oven about 30 minutes or until instant read thermometer inserted into lamb, but not touching bone, registers 145 degrees F. for medium or to desired doneness.
3. Place lamb in carving board; tent with foil. Let stand 10 minutes for easier slicing. Internal temperature will continue to rise about 5 to 10 degrees during stand time. Slice between ribs into individual chops with large carving knife. Garnish with additional fresh herbs and mango slices, if desired. Serve immediately.
Makes 4 Servings

Cranberry-Orange Game Hens

Game Hens
4 small Cornish game hens
1 carrot, finely diced
1 stalk celery, finely diced
2 cups bread stuffing mix
1 teaspoon poultry seasoning
1 cup chicken stock or broth
Salt and pepper

Sauce
1 cup fresh or frozen cranberries, chopped
1 (12-oz) jar, sweet orange marmalade
¼ cup water
1 teaspoon lemon juice
Lemon wedges, optional

Directions

1. Preheat oven to 400 degrees F. Trim as much fat as possible from game hens. Combine carrots, celery, stuffing mix, poultry seasoning and chicken stock, Season stuffing with salt and pepper, to taste. Fill cavity of each game hen with stuffing; Bake for 45 minutes.
2. Meanwhile, **prepare sauce**. In a medium saucepan, combine all ingredients. Cook over medium heat for 5 to 8 minutes or until cranberries have released their juice; set aside.
3. Remove game hens from oven. Spread sauce over top and sides of hens. Reserve any extra sauce to serve later with hens. Return hens to oven and continue baking 10 to 15 minutes.

To Serve: Place game hens on 4 serving plates. Spoon some onto each plate. Spoon additional sauce over hens Garnish with lemon wedges, if desired.
Makes 4 servings

Prime Rib with Horseradish Cream Sauce

Horseradish Cream Sauce
3 garlic cloves, minced
1 teaspoon black pepper
3 rib standing roast, trimmed, (6 to7 lbs)

Directions

1. Prepare **Horseradish Cream Sauce**. Preheat oven to 450 degrees F. Combine garlic and pepper, rub over surface of roast.
2. Place roast bone side down in shallow roasting pan. Insert meat thermometer in thickest part of roast, not touching bone or fat. Roast 15 minutes.
3. Reduce oven temperature to 325 degrees F. Roast 20 minutes per pound or until internal temperature is 145 degrees F. for medium.
4. When roast has reached desired temperature; transfer to cutting board; tent with foil, let stand 15 to 20 minutes to allow for easier carving. Temperature of roast will continue to rise about 10 degrees F. during standing time. Serve with Horseradish Cream Sauce.
Makes 8 Servings

Horseradish Cream Sauce

1 cup whipping cream
¼ cup prepared horseradish, undrained
2 teaspoons balsamic or red wine vinegar
1 teaspoon dry mustard

¼ teaspoon sugar
1/8 teaspoon salt

Directions

Beat cream until soft peaks form. Do not overbeat. In a medium bowl; combine horseradish, vinegar, mustard, sugar and salt. Fold whipped cream into horseradish mixture. Cover and refrigerate at least 1 hour. Sauce may be made up to 8 hours before serving
Makes 1 ½ cups
Note: For extra flavor, rub with fresh herbs, such as chopped thyme leaves and rosemary, onto the meat before roasting.

Herb-Crusted Roast Beef

1 boneless rump roast (4 ½ to 5-lbs)
2 garlic cloves, minced
2 Tablespoons; Dijon mustard
2 Tablespoons lemon juice
2 Tablespoons olive oil
2 Tablespoons Worcestershire sauce
1 Tablespoon dried parsley flakes
1 teaspoon dried basil
1 teaspoon salt
1 teaspoon coarsely ground pepper
½ teaspoon dried tarragon
½ teaspoon dried thyme
2 1/3 cups water, divided
2 teaspoons beef bouillon granules
¼ to 1/3 cup all-purpose flour

Directions

1. Place beef fat side down in an ungreased roasting pan. Combine the next 5 ingredients; pour over roast. Combine parsley, basil, salt, pepper, tarragon and thyme; rub over roast.
2. Bake, uncovered, at 325 degrees F. for 1 ¾ hours to 2 ¼ hours or until roast reaches desired doneness (for rare, meat thermometer should read 140 degrees F. Medium 160 degrees F. Well done 170 degrees F,) remove to a warm serving platter; let stand for 10 to 15 minutes.
3. Meanwhile, add 2 cups water and bouillon to pan drippings; bring to a boil. Combine flour and remaining water until smooth; gradually add to pan. Cook stirring until bubbly and thickened. Slice roast; serve with gravy,
Makes 10 to 12 Servings

Sunshine-Glazed Ham

1 (10 to 12 lb.) uncooked ham
Whole cloves
1 (6-oz) can frozen orange juice concentrate, thawed and undiluted
½ cup molasses
¼ cup prepared mustard
1 Tablespoon grated orange peel
Peach halves, optional
Fresh parsley sprigs, optional

Directions

1. Preheat oven to 325 degrees F. Remove skin from ham. Score fat in a diamond design, and stud with cloves. Place ham in

shallow baking pan, fat side up. Insert meat thermometer, making sure it does not touch fat or bone.
2. Combine next 4 ingredients, stirring well; brush on ham. Bake uncovered, for 3 to 4 hours or until meat thermometer registers 160 degrees F; baste every 30 minutes with juice mixture. Garnish with peach halves and parsley, if desired
Makes 20 Servings

Ham Royale

¾ cup orange juice
½ cup dry sherry
1 cup firmly packed brown sugar
2 Tablespoons prepared mustard
¼ teaspoon ground cloves
1 (5 to 6 lbs.) fully cooked ham half
1 Tablespoon cornstarch
1 Tablespoon water

Directions

1. Combine first 5 ingredients in a small bowl. Stir well. Place ham in a shallow baking pan; prick thoroughly with a fork. Pour orange juice mixture over ham; marinate 2 hours in refrigerator, turning ham occasionally.
2. Preheat oven to 325 degrees F. Place ham, fat side up, in baking pan along with marinade; insert meat thermometer, making sure it does not touch fat or bone. Bake uncovered for 1 ½ to 2 hours or until meat thermometer registers 140 degrees F., basting every 30 minutes with marinade. Remove ham from baking pan; reserve 1 cup marinade

3. Combine cornstarch and water in a small saucepan, mixing well. Add the reserved marinade, and bring to a boil. Boil 1 minute, and remove from heat. Serve sauce with sliced ham. Makes 10 to 12 Servings

Crown Roast with Cranberry-Pecan Stuffing

1 Tablespoon salt
1 Tablespoon black pepper
2 teaspoons dried thyme
1 (16-rib) crown pork roast, trimmed
2 cups Cranberry-pecan Stuffing
¼ cup butter or margarine
1/3 cup all-purpose flour
2 (14 ½ -oz.) cans chicken broth
2 Tablespoons orange liqueur
2 Tablespoons grated orange peel
¼ teaspoon salt
¼ teaspoon pepper
Garnishes: Kumquat leaves, sugared kumquats, grape clusters, or crab apples, if desired

Directions

1. Combine first 3 ingredients; rub over all sides of roast.
2. Fold a piece of foil into an 8-inch square; place on a rack in a roasting pan. Place roast, bone ends up, on foil lined rack.
3. Bake at 350 degrees F. for 1 hour.

4. Spoon 2 cups Cranberry-Pecan Stuffing into the center of the roast; cover with a 12-inch square of heavy-duty foil, and fold over tips of ribs.
5. Bake at 350 degrees F, for 1 ½ hours or until a meat thermometer registers 160 degrees F. Remove foil; let stand 15 minutes before slicing.
6. Pour pan drippings into a skillet; add butter and cook over medium heat until butter melts. Add flour, whisking until smooth; cook whisking constantly, until caramel colored.
7. Stir in chicken broth and next 4 ingredients; cook, whisking constantly; until smooth and thickened. Serve with roast. Garnish if desired
Makes 12 Servings

Cranberry-Pecan Stuffing

This stuffing can be made the day before. Just; place in a large bowl and refrigerate until ready to bake, if not preparing a roast, spoon all the stuffing; Into 2 lightly greased 11x7x1½ –inch baking pans, bake as directed.

2 cups dried cranberries
1 cup orange liqueur
2 pounds mild ground pork sausage
4 cups coarsely chopped celery
1 ½ cups chopped onion
½ cup butter or margarine
1 (14 ½ -oz) can chicken broth
1 teaspoon salt
½ teaspoon pepper
1 teaspoon thyme
2 (16-oz) pkg pork stuffing mix
2 Tablespoons grated orange peel
2 cups chopped pecans

Directions

1. In a small saucepan, combine cranberries and liqueur; bring to a boil over medium-high heat. Remove from heat, set aside.
2. In a large skillet, brown sausage, stirring until it crumbles; drain, reserving 2 Tablespoons drippings in skillet. Set aside.
3. Add celery and onions to reserved drippings; cook over medium high heat 10 minutes, stirring constantly. Add butter, chicken broth, salt, pepper and thyme; cook stirring constantly, 3 minutes or until butter melts.
4. In a large bowl, combine cranberry mixture, sausage and stuffing mix and seasoning packets, orange peel and pecans, stir well.

5. Spoon 2 cups stuffing into the center of crown pork roast: spoon remaining stuffing into lightly greased 13 x 9 x 2-inch baking pan.
6. Cover and bake at 350 degrees F. for 20 minutes; uncover and bake 10 additional minutes or until lightly browned.
Makes 12 Servings

Pork Roast with Corn Bread & Oyster Stuffing

1 (5 to 7 lbs.) pork loin roast
2 Tablespoons butter or margarine
½ cup chopped onion
½ cup chopped celery
2 garlic clove, minced
½ teaspoon funnel seeds, crushed
1 teaspoon Tabasco hot pepper sauce
½ teaspoon salt
2 cups packaged corn bread stuffing mix
1 (8-oz) can oysters, undrained, chopped

Directions

1. Preheat oven to 325 degrees F. Make a slit in the back of each chop on the pork loin. In a large saucepan melt butter; add onion, celery, garlic and fennel seeds. Cook 5 minutes or until vegetables are tender, stir in Tabasco sauce and salt. Add stuffing mix, oysters and oyster liquid; toss to mix well.
2. Stuff corn bread mixture; into slits in pork roast. (Any left-over stuffing may be baked in covered baking dish during last 30 minutes of roasting.)
3. Place pork roast in shallow roasting pan. Cook 30 to 35 minutes per pound or until instant-read thermometer registers

170 degrees F. Transfer to serving platter. Let stand 15 minutes before carving.
Makes 12 Servings

Note: Have your butcher-crack the bone of pork loin roast.

-
-
-
-

Simple Roast Duckling

1 (4-pound) cleaned duckling (fresh or frozen) thawed
1 ½ Tablespoons five-spice seasoning powder
1 teaspoon salt
4 cups rock salt

Directions

1. Preheat oven to 500 degrees F.

2. Remove giblets and neck from duckling; reserve for another use. Rinse duckling under cold water; pat dry. Trim excess fat. Starting at neck cavity; loosen skin from breast and drumsticks, by inserting fingers and pushing hand between skin and meat.
3. Combine five-spice powder and 1 teaspoon salt. Sprinkle spice mixture under loosened skin; rub into body cavity. Tie ends of legs together with string. Lift wing tips up and over back; tuck under duckling.
4. Spread rock salt in bottom of a shallow roasting pan. Place duckling, breast side up, on rock salt. Pierce skin several times with a meat fork. Insert a meat thermometer into meaty part of thigh; make sure not to touch bone.

5. Bake in preheated oven for 45 minutes or until thermometer registers 180 degrees F. Cover loosely with foil; let stand 10 minutes. Discard skin.
Makes 4 (3-oz) servings

Roast Turkey with Chestnut Stuffing

If you can't find fresh chestnuts, use 4-oz dried chestnuts and soak them over night.

8-10 pound turkey, defrost if frozen
3 Tablespoons butter, softened

For the Chestnut Stuffing
6 bacon slices, diced
8 oz fresh chestnuts, cooked, peeled, chopped
1 cup fresh white bread crumbs
1 egg, beaten
½ bunch watercress, trimmed and finely chopped
Salt and pepper

Directions

1. For the Dressing: Place bacon in nonstick sauté pan over low heat until fat is released. Add chestnuts and cook over medium heat for 10 minutes, or until, bacon is crisp. Add bread crumbs.
2. Transfer to a bowl and let cool. Add egg, watercress, salt and pepper, mix well.
3. Preheat oven to 350 degrees F. Spoon the cold stuffing into the neck end of the turkey, pull the skin over, and secure with a skewer. Twist the wing tips up and over; tie the wings and legs with string.

4. Spread butter over turkey, sprinkle with salt and pepper, place turkey breast side up, on a rack in a roasting pan. Insert a thermometer into the thickest part of the thigh, away from the bone.

5. Roast for 3 to 3 ½ hours, until the juices run clear when a skewer inserted in thigh, or thermometer reads 185 degrees F. If the turkey browns before it's cooked, cover with foil and continue roasting. Let stand, wrapped in foil, while you make the gravy.

For Turkey Gravy: Tilt pan so the juices settle in one corner, and scoop off most of the fat. Place the roasting pan on the burner, over medium heat.

Sprinkle 2 teaspoons flour over the juices in the pan and whisk with a wire whisk over medium heat for 2 to 3 minutes until the flour browns a little,

Pour in 1 ¼ cups hot stock, bring to a boil, whisking constantly. If you desire ass 4 Tablespoons red or white wine; whisk to mix. Simmer for 2 minutes, check seasoning, and adjust seasonings as desired

Cajun Deep-Fried Turkey

1/3 cup kosher salt
3 Tablespoons onion powder
3 Tablespoons black pepper
3 Tablespoons white pepper
2 Tablespoons sweet basil
2 Teaspoons bay leaves, ground
1 Tablespoon cayenne pepper
2 teaspoons filé powder
3 Tablespoons garlic powder

1 ½ Tablespoons paprika
1 (10-12 lbs) Whole Turkey, not self-basting
4 to 5 Gallons peanut oil

Directions

1. In a bowl, combine salt, herbs and peppers together. Mix until well blended. Use 1/2 to 2/3 cup for a 10-12 pound turkey. Remainder may be stored for several months in an airtight covered jar.
2. Remove the giblets and neck, rinse the turkey well with cold water and pat dry thoroughly with paper towels. Take care to dry inside cavities. Place in a large pan and rub the interior and exterior of the bird with seasoning mix. For good oil circulation through the cavity, (do not truss or tie legs together). Cut off the wing tips and tail as they could get caught in the fryer basket. Cover pan and place in refrigerator overnight.
3. Heat peanut oil in a turkey fryer or a very, very large stockpot to 375 degrees F. Lower turkey into hot oil, very carefully, making sure it is fully submerged. Fry turkey for 3 to 4 minutes per pound or until the internal temperature of the breast reaches 155 degrees F.   On an instant-read thermometer, about 45 minutes. Carefully remove the turkey from the oil and let it rest and drain on a wire rack, about 30 minutes. The internal temperature will rise to 165 degrees F while resting. Remove turkey from oil and drain on rack.
4. Remove turkey from the rack and place on a serving platter. Allow to rest for 20 minutes before carving.
NOTE: Use only oils with high smoke points, such as peanut, canola or safflower oil. To determine the correct amount of oil, place the turkey in the pot before adding seasoning and add water until turkey is covered. Take turkey out of the water before marking the oil level. Measure the amount of water and use a corresponding amount of oil. Dry the pot thoroughly of all water.

Always fry your Turkey outside away from buildings on a dirt or grassy area.

Turkey in a Bag

10 to 12 pounds whole turkey
Salt and pepper to taste
1 Tablespoon thyme
2 teaspoons rosemary, crushed
1 teaspoon rubbed sage, optional
2 Tablespoons butter
Olive oil cooking spray
2 tablespoons all-purpose flour
5 stalks celery
2 large onions, quartered

Directions

1. Preheat oven to 350 degrees F.
2. Rinse turkey and remove giblets.
3. Season cavity with, thyme, rosemary, sage, salt and pepper to taste. With fingers loosen skin from breast meat, Press slices of cold butter between skin and breast meat. Spray skin with olive oil spray, if desired
Sprinkle the bottom of a turkey size oven bag with flour. Place turkey, celery and onions in the bag. Seal bag, with a fork piece several holes in bag.
4. Bake 3 to 3 ½ hours, or until internal temperature of the thigh meat reaches 180 degrees F. Let stand 20 minutes before carving.

Turkey Gravy

1 ¼ pounds giblets and neck from turkey
1 cup chopped onion
1 cup chopped celery
1 cup chopped carrots
1 pinch ground black pepper, or to taste
2 (1.2 ounce) packages dry turkey gravy mix
3 (14.5 ounce) cans chicken broth, or more as needed
2 cups turkey drippings
1/4 cup quick-mixing flour (such as Wondra)

Directions

1. Place the giblets and turkey neck into a large saucepan with onion, celery, carrots, pepper, and turkey gravy mix. Pour the chicken broth over the mixture, bring to a simmer over medium-low heat, and simmer for 40 minutes. Remove the turkey liver and set aside. Allow the stock to simmer for 2 more hours. Stock should equal about 3 cups; add more chicken broth if necessary. Remove the giblets and chop, chop the liver if desired; set aside,. Strain the stock into a saucepan; discard bones and vegetables.
2. When the turkey is finished roasting, pour the drippings into a fat separator or bowl, and skim off the fat. In a bowl, whisk the quick-mixing flour with the pan drippings until smooth, and then whisk the flour mixture into the stock. Bring the gravy mixture to a simmer over medium heat, whisking constantly, and add the chopped giblets, if desired.
Makes about 5 cups

Turkey Breast Stuffed with Wild Rice & Cranberries

4 cups cooked wild rice
¾ cup onion, finely chopped
½ cup dried cranberries
1/3 cup slivered almonds
2 medium golden delicious apples, peeled or unpeeled, coarsely chopped (2 cups)
1 boneless whole turkey breast (4 to 5 lbs.) thawed if frozen.

Directions

In a medium bowl, mix all ingredients except turkey. Cut turkey into slices at 1-inch intervals about ¾ the way through, forming deep pockets.
Place turkey in 3 ½ qt or larger slow cooker. Stuff pockets with wild rice mixture. Place remaining rice mixture around edges of cooker.
Cover and cook on Low 8 to 10 hours, until turkey is no longer pink inside.
Makes 10 Servings

Turkey in Cranberry Leek Sauce

1 Tablespoon olive oil
1 skin and bone in turkey breast. (About 1½ lbs.)
2 medium leeks, white and light green part only, rinsed well and thinly sliced
2 garlic cloves, minced
2 teaspoons dried thyme leaves
½ teaspoon black peppercorns
1 Tablespoon all-purpose flour
1 Cup chicken or turkey broth
Salt, optional
½ cup dried cranberries
2 Tablespoons parsley, finely chopped

Directions

In a large nonstick skillet, heat oil over medium-high heat. Add turkey breast, skin side down, cook until browned, about 4 minutes. Transfer to slow cooker.
Add leeks to skillet and cook, stirring over medium-high heat, until softened, about 5 minutes. Add garlic, thyme and peppercorns, cook stirring 1 minute. Add broth, flour and cook, stirring until mixture begins to thicken, about 2 minutes. Season with salt to taste: if using. Stir in cranberries.
Transfer sauce to slow cooker, covering turkey with sauce. Cover and cook on High 2 ½ to 3 hours or on Low 5 ½ to 6 hours, until an instant-read thermometer inserted into center of breast registers 175 degrees F. To serve: transfer to a platter and garnish with parsley.
Makes 6 Servings

Sweet Potato Stuffing

½ cup chopped celery, including tops

1 medium onion, chopped
¼ cup butter (½ stick)
6 cups dry bread crumbs
1 large sweet potato, cooked, peeled, finely chopped
½ cup chicken broth
¼ cup chopped toasted pecans
½ teaspoon poultry seasoning
¼ teaspoon rubbed sage
½ teaspoon salt
¼ teaspoon black or white pepper

Directions

In heavy skillet, melt butter over medium heat; sauté celery and onion until tender, stirring frequently. Add remaining ingredients and toss gently to coat. Grease a 4 to 5 quart and fill with stuffing, ½ to ¾ full. Cover crock-pot and cook on Low for 4-5 hours until stuffing is hot.
Makes 6-8 Servings

Slow-Cooker Turkey

3 celery stalks, chopped
1 small onion, chopped
3 garlic cloves, minced
1/2 cup chicken broth
1 (6 -7 lbs) bone-in turkey breast
1 (1 ounce) envelope dry onion soup mix
1 Tablespoon butter

Directions

1. Place celery, onion, minced garlic and chicken broth on bottom of slow cooker.

2. Rinse the turkey breast and pat dry. Cut off any excess skin, but leave the skin covering the breast. Rub onion soup mix all over outside and lifting the skin, directly on the meat of the turkey.
3. Place in a slow cooker, drizzle with 1 Tablespoon butter; Cover, and cook on High for 1 hour, then set to Low, and cook for 7 hours.

Stuffing Recipes

Bread Stuffing with Onions and Celery

1 stick (8-oz) unsalted butter
2 medium onions, chopped
3 medium celery ribs, chopped
½ cup chopped celery leaves, (from inner ribs)
1 pound firm white sandwich b read, cut into ¼-inch cubes and dried over night or in the oven or 10 cups plain bread croutons.
¼ cup fresh parsley, chopped
2 teaspoons poultry seasoning
1 ½ teaspoons salt
½ teaspoons freshly ground black pepper
1 ½ to 2 cups turkey or chicken broth

Directions

Preheat oven to 350 degrees F.
In a large skillet, melt the butter over medium heat. Add onions, celery and celery leaves. Stirring often until the onions are golden, about 8 minutes.

Transfer celery, onion and butter into a large bowl. Mix in the bread cubes, parsley, poultry seasoning, salt and pepper. Gradually stir in about 1½ cups of broth, until the stuffing is evenly moistened but not soggy. Use as a stuffing; or place in a

lightly buttered casserole, drizzle with ½ cup broth, cover, and bake for 30 to 40 minutes; for a crispy crust bake uncovered for 10 minutes.
Makes 10 cups

Oyster Stuffing

Drain 2 (8-oz) containers of oysters and reserve juice.(Or shuck 24 oysters, opening them over a fine wire sieve placed over a bowl to catch the juices.)If the oysters are large, cut them into 2 or 3 pieces. Add the oyster <u>to Bread stuffing</u> along with the bread cubes. Add enough turkey or chicken broth to the reserved oyster juices to make 1 ½ cups and use to moisten the stuffing mixture.

Sausage and Bread Stuffing

In a skillet over medium heat, cook 1 pound bulk pork breakfast sausage, breaking up the meat with a spoon, until cooked through, about 10 minutes. Add to <u>bread stuffing</u> (above) with the bread cubes and mix. Reduce the salt to 1 teaspoon.

Chapter 4: Side Dishes

Choosing sides is often the most difficult part of menu planning, why not try something new? Expand your choices to include Mediterranean caramelized onions, Portabella mushrooms to Thai Green Bean Casserole

Green Beans with Almonds

2 pounds fresh green beans
2 quarts water
1 teaspoon salt
¼ cups butter or margarine
Salt and pepper to taste
2/3 cup sliced almonds, toasted

Directions

1. Wash beans; trim ends, remove strings. Cut diagonally into 3-inch pieces. Combine water and 1 teaspoon salt, bring to a boil. Add beans. Cook uncovered, 4 to 5 minutes, or just until crisp tender. Drain beans, and plunge into ice water; drain.

2. Melt butter in a large skillet; add the beans, sauté 2 to 3 minutes or until thoroughly heated. Sprinkle with salt, pepper and almonds.
Makes 8 to 10 Servings

Tangerine Sweet Potatoes

9 cups peeled, thinly sliced sweet potatoes (about 2 ½ lbs)
8 lemon slices
Vegetable cooking spray
2/3 cup firmly packed brown sugar
1 Tablespoon grated tangerine or orange peel
½ cup fresh tangerine or orange juice
2 Tablespoons margarine, melted

Directions

Preheat oven to 400 degrees F. Spray 13 x 9-inch baking dish with vegetable cooking spray.

Arrange sweet potatoes and lemon slices in prepared baking dish. Combine brown sugar, grated tangerine peel, tangerine juice and margarine. Drizzle sugar mixture over sweet potatoes; cover with foil. Bake for 35 minutes. Uncover potatoes and stir well; bake an additional 30 minutes.
Makes 12- ½ cup Servings

Twice Baked Sweet Potatoes

A variation on twice-baked potatoes, these are an eye-catching takeoff on a sweet potato casserole. The sweet potatoes flesh is pureed with butter and milk, returned to the hollowed-out shells, and topped with mini marshmallows before the final baking.
You can puree the potatoes in a blender or food processor; use the blender for an especially silky texture

4 medium sweet potatoes, washed and halved lengthwise
1/3 cup buttermilk

1/3 cup milk or as needed
4 Tablespoons (½ stick) butter
Freshly ground black pepper
½ cup miniature marshmallows for garnish

Directions

1. Adjust oven rack to lowest position. Preheat oven to 400 degrees F.
2. Place potatoes cut side down on foil or parchment-lined baking sheet. Bake until fork-tender, about 30 minutes. Let cool slightly.
3. Holding a potato half with a pot holder, scoop potato flesh into a blender or food processor, leaving a ¼ - inch shell with remaining potato, set shells aside.
4. With motor running, gradually add both milks to potatoes. Add butter, then process, adding more milk if necessary, until potatoes are silky smooth. Add salt and pepper to taste.
5. Spoon puree back into potato shells. Sprinkle marshmallows over potatoes. Place on baking sheet and bake until potatoes are hot and marshmallows are golden brown, 10 to 12 minutes. Serve hot.
Makes 8 Servings

Butterbeans with Bacon and Green Onions

2 (10-oz) pkgs. frozen butterbeans
6 lean bacon slices
4 green onions, chopped
2 garlic cloves, minced
½ cup chopped fresh parsley
½ teaspoon salt
½ teaspoon pepper

Directions

1. Cook beans according to package directions, set aside.
2. Cook bacon in a large skillet over medium-high heat until crisp; remove bacon, reserving drippings in skillet. Crumble bacon, set aside.
3. Cook green onions and garlic in drippings until tender, stirring often. Stir in beans, chopped parsley, salt and pepper, cook just until thoroughly heated. Sprinkle with crumbled bacon.
Makes 8 to 10 Servings

Mediterranean Caramelized Onions

4 medium onions (about 1½ lbs.)
1½ teaspoons salt
½ teaspoon pepper
Dash saffron
1 Tablespoon chopped fresh parsley
1 Tablespoon chopped fresh chives
1 Tablespoon chopped fresh thyme
1 teaspoon butter or margarine
1 teaspoon olive oil

Directions

1. Cut onions into ¼ -inch thick slices, and separate into rings. Combine onions, salt, pepper, saffron, parsley, chives and thyme, tossing to coat.
2. Melt butter in a large heavy skillet over medium heat; add oil and onion and cook, stirring constantly, 25 minutes or until onions are lightly browned and tender.
Makes 4 to 6 servings

Sautéed Portobello Mushrooms

3 pounds fresh Portobello mushrooms
12 garlic cloves, minced
2/3 cup olive oil
¾ cup chopped fresh Italian parsley, divided
¼ teaspoon salt
1/8 teaspoon pepper

Directions

1. Cut mushrooms into ¼ - inch thick slices.
2. Cook 6 minced garlic cloves in 1/3 cup olive oil in an extra large skillet over medium heat until tender, stirring often. Add half the mushroom slices and ¼ cup parsley; cook 4 to 5 minutes, or until tender and browned, turning once. Transfer to a serving dish; sprinkle with half of each salt and pepper. Repeat procedure; sprinkle remaining ¼ cup parsley, serve immediately. Makes 12 servings

Note: Substitute 3 pounds fresh mushrooms for the Portobello. Do not slice; stir constantly during cooking.

Green Beans, Walnut and Feta Salad

1 cup coarsely chopped walnuts
¾ cup olive oil
¼ cup white wine vinegar
1 Tablespoon chopped fresh dill
½ teaspoon minced garlic
¼ teaspoon salt
¼ teaspoon pepper
1 1/3 pounds fresh green beans
1 small purple onion, thinly slices

1 (4-oz) pkg. crumbled Feta cheese

Directions

1. Place walnuts in shallow pan, bake at 350 degrees F. for 5 to 10 minutes or until toasted, stirring occasionally; set aside.
2. Combine next 6 ingredients; cover and chill,
3. Cut green beans into thirds, and arrange in a steaming basket over boiling water. Cover and steam for 15 minutes or until crisp-tender. Immediately plunge into ice cold water, to stop the cooking process; drain and pat dry.
4. Combine walnuts, beans, onion and cheese in a large bowl. Cover and chill.
5. Pour oil mixture over bean mixture 1 hour before serving; toss just before serving.
Makes 6 Servings

Tangy Mixed Vegetables

1 (8-oz) pkg. sliced fresh mushrooms
1 green bell pepper, cut into 1-inch pieces
1 medium onion, chopped
1 (8-oz) can pineapple chunks, undrained
4 medium carrots, peeled and sliced
½ teaspoon ground ginger
½ teaspoon curry powder
½ teaspoon dried basil
1 (8-oz) can sliced water chestnuts, drained
1 Tablespoon brown sugar
¼ teaspoon salt

Directions

1. In a large nonstick skillet, cook mushrooms, bell pepper and onion for 5 minutes or until tender, stirring often. Drain and set aside.
2. Drain pineapple, reserve juice. Pour juice into skillet; set pineapple chunks aside. Add carrots, ground ginger, curry powder and basil to the juice; bring to a boil. Cover, reduce heat and simmer 10 to 15 minutes or until carrots are tender.
3. Stir in mushroom mixture, pineapple chunks, water chestnuts and remaining ingredients; cook over medium-high heat until thoroughly heated.
Makes 4 Servings

Wild Rice with Apricots and Cranberries

½ cup uncooked wild rice, rinsed and drained
3 cups chicken broth, divided
1 cup apple juice
¾ cup uncooked long-grain rice
½ cup golden raisins
½ cup chopped dried apricots
½ cup dried cranberries
2 Tablespoons butter
¾ cup chopped onion
½ cup coarsely chopped pecans
1/3 cup chopped fresh parsley

Directions

1. Combine wild rice, 1 ½ cups chicken broth and apple juice in 2-quart saucepan. Bring to a boil over medium-high heat. Reduce heat to low; simmer, covered, about 1 hour or until rice is tender. Drain; set aside.

2. Combine white rice and remaining 1 ½ cups broth in separate 2-quart saucepan. Bring to a boil over medium high heat. Reduce heat to low; simmer, covered, 12 to 15 minutes.
3. Stir in raisins, apricots and cranberries; simmer 5 minutes or until rice is tender and fluffy and liquid is absorbed. Remove from heat. Let stand, covered, 5 minutes or until fruit is tender; set aside.
4. In a large skillet melt butter over medium heat. Add onion; cook and stir 5 to 6 minutes or until tender. Stir in pecans. Cook and stir 2 minutes.
5. Add wild rice and white rice mixtures to skillet. Stir in parsley; cook and stir over medium heat about 2 minutes or until heated through.
Garnish with fresh thyme, orange slices and whole cranberries, if desired.
Makes 6 to 8 Servings

Golden Apples and Yams

2 large yams or sweet potatoes
2 Golden Delicious Apples, cored and sliced crosswise into rings
¼ firmly packed brown sugar
1 teaspoon cornstarch
1/8 teaspoon ground cloves
½ cup orange juice
2 Tablespoon chopped pecans or walnuts

Directions

1. Preheat oven to 400 degrees F. Bake yams 50 minutes or until soft but still hold their shape. Let yams cool enough to handle. Reduce oven temperature to 350 degrees F.

2. Peel and slice yams crosswise. In shallow 1-quart baking dish, alternate apple rings and yam slices, over lapping edges slightly. In a small sauce pan combine sugar, cornstarch and cloves; stir in orange juice and mix well. Heat orange juice mixture over medium heat, stirring, until thickened; pour over apples and yams. Sprinkle with nuts; Bake 20 minutes or until apples and yams are tender.
Makes 6 Servings

Green Beans with Blue Cheese

1 (20 ounces) frozen cut green beans
½ jar (3-oz) roasted red pepper Strips drained and slivered
1/8 teaspoon salt
1/8 teaspoon white pepper
4 ounces cream cheese
½ cup milk
3 ounces crumbled blue cheese
½ cup Italian-style bread crumbs
1 Tablespoon butter, melted

Directions

1. Preheat oven to 350 degrees F. Spray 2-quart oval casserole with nonstick cooking spray.
2. Combine green beans, red pepper strips, salt and pepper, in prepared dish.
3. Place cream cheese and milk in a small saucepan; cook and stir until cheese is melted. Add blue cheese; Stir only until combined. Pour cheese mixture over green bean mixture and stir until green beans are coated.
4. Combine bread crumbs and butter in a small bowl; sprinkle evenly over casserole.

5. Bake, uncovered, 20 minutes or until hot and bubbly.
Makes 4 servings

Marinated Brussels Sprouts

3 (10-oz) pkg. frozen Brussels sprouts, thawed
½ cup olive oil
¼ cup white vinegar
1 (2-oz) jar sliced pimiento, drained
2 Tablespoons diced onion
2 Tablespoons minced fresh parsley
1 teaspoon dried thyme
1 teaspoon pepper
¾ teaspoon salt

Directions

1. Cook Brussels sprouts according to package directions, omitting salt and drain well.
2. Whisk oil and remaining ingredients until blended; pour over Brussels sprouts, stirring gently to coat Cover and chill 2 hours.
Makes 8 Servings

Note: You can substitute 2 pounds fresh Brussels sprouts for frozen Brussels sprouts. Cook fresh Brussels sprouts in 1 cup boiling water for 8 minutes or until tender.

Broccoli with Parmesan Sauce

1 ½ pounds fresh broccoli
1 cup water
Vegetable cooking spray
¼ cup chopped red pepper
¼ cup chopped onion
1 Tablespoon margarine
2 teaspoons all-purpose flour
¾ cup milk
2 ounces cream cheese
¼ cup grated parmesan cheese
¼ teaspoon garlic powder

Directions

1. Remove tough ends from lower broccoli stalks, and wash thoroughly. Cut into spears. Place broccoli into spears. Place broccoli in a Dutch oven, add water. Bring to a boil, cover, reduce heat, and simmer 10 to 15 minutes or until tender-crisp. Drain; arrange broccoli on a serving platter, keep warm.
2. Coat large nonstick skillet with cooking spray, place over medium heat until hot. Add red pepper and onion; cook, stirring constantly, until tender. Remove from skillet, and set aside.
3. Melt margarine in skillet, stir in flour. Gradually add milk. Cook; stirring constantly: Until slightly thickened. Add reserved onion and red pepper, cream cheese, parmesan cheese and garlic powder; cook over low heat. Stirring constantly: until smooth and thoroughly heated. Spoon over broccoli and Serve immediately
Makes 6 servings

Brussels Sprouts with Pecans

1 pound fresh Brussels sprouts
1 ½ cups water
Vegetable cooking oil
1 teaspoon margarine
1 teaspoon cooking oil
¼ pound fresh mushrooms, sliced
¼ cup coarsely chopped pecans
¼ teaspoon salt
1/8 teaspoon pepper
¼ cup soft whole wheat breadcrumbs
2 Tablespoons grated parmesan cheese

Directions

1. Wash Brussels sprouts thoroughly, remove any discolored leaves. Cut off stem ends, and slash bottom of each sprout with a shallow X.
2. Place Brussels sprouts and water in a medium saucepan; bring to a boil. Cover, reduce heat, and simmer 8 to 10 minutes or until tender-crisp. Drain and set aside.
3. Coat a large nonstick skillet with cooking spray, add margarine and oil. Place over medium high heat until hot. Add mushrooms and pecans, cook, stirring constantly, until mushrooms are tender. Stir in Brussels sprouts. Transfer mixture to an 11 x 7 x 2 inch baking dish.
4. Combine salt, pepper, breadcrumbs and parmesan cheese, stirring well; sprinkle breadcrumb mixture over Brussels sprouts. Broil 4 inches from heat 2 to 3 minutes or until breadcrumbs are golden.
Makes 6 servings

Steamed Zucchini with Green Onions

4 zucchini, (about 2 pounds), cut diagonally into ¼ -inch thick rounds
1 tablespoon olive oil
2 tablespoons green onions, thinly sliced
3 Tablespoons Parmesan cheese
Coarse salt and ground pepper

Directions

1. Fill a large skillet with just enough water to cover bottom (about ¼ cup). Bring to a simmer over medium heat. Add zucchini. Cook; covered, until tender, 3 to 4 minutes. Drain, transfer to a medium bowl.
2. Drizzle; zucchini with oil; sprinkle with green onions, parmesan cheese, Season with salt and pepper; toss to combine. Makes 5 to 6 Servings

Cheesy Mashed Potatoes with Gouda

1 pound red-skin potatoes cut into 1 ½ inch pieces
1 pound russet potatoes, peeled and cut into 1 ½ inch pieces
¾ cup half-and-half, light cream, or whipping cream
2 cups finely shredded Gouda cheese (8 ounces)
2 green onions or chives
Salt
Freshly ground black pepper

Directions

1. In a 4- to 5-quart Dutch oven or saucepan cook potatoes, covered, in lightly salted boiling water to cover for 20 to 25 minutes or until tender; drain. Return potatoes to Dutch oven.

2. Meanwhile, thinly slice green onions, set aside.
3. Add half-and-half to cooked potatoes. Mash with a potato masher or an electric mixer on low speed until nearly smooth. Stir in 1 ½ cups of the cheese Season to taste with salt and pepper
4. Transfer mashed potatoes to a serving dish. Sprinkle with green or chives onions and the remaining ½ cup cheese.
Makes 8 Servings

Garlic Mashed Potatoes

2 ½ pounds russet or Yukon potatoes
1 whole garlic bulb
1 Tablespoon olive oil
½ cup sour cream
2 Tablespoons (¼ stick) butter
1/8 teaspoon salt
1/8 teaspoon pepper
Fresh chives

Directions

1. Preheat oven to 375 degrees F. Peel potatoes and cut into even pieces. Place in a large saucepan of lightly salted water. Bring to a boil. Reduce heat and simmer, about 20 minutes.
2. Meanwhile, separate garlic cloves, but do not peel them. Place in a bowl, add olive oil and toss to coat. Place on a baking sheet and roast until softened, about 10 minutes, allow to cool slightly
3. Drain potatoes and return to saucepan. Mash slightly. Add sour cream and butter. Quickly squeeze pulp from garlic cloves into potatoes. Add salt and pepper.

4. Mash potatoes until combined and smooth. Transfer to a serving bowl. Cut chives into small pieces. Sprinkle over mashed potatoes; serve
Makes 4 servings

Au Gratin Potatoes

4 cups thinly sliced potatoes
1 medium onion, chopped
¼ cup butter
1 tablespoon all-purpose flour
1 teaspoon salt
¼ teaspoon pepper
2 cups milk
2 cups (8 ounces) shredded sharp cheddar cheese, divided
¼ cup fine dry bread crumbs
Paprika

Directions

1. Preheat oven to 325 degrees F.
2. In a 2 quart saucepan, sauté onion in butter until tender. Stir in flour, salt and pepper; cook over low heat until mixture is bubbly, stirring constantly. Remove from heat; gradually stir in milk and 1 ½ cups cheese. Bring to a boil, stirring constantly; cook for 1 minute.
3. In an ungreased 1 ½ quart casserole dish, place potatoes; cover with cheese sauce.
4. Bake, uncovered, for 1 hour.
5. Mix remaining cheese and bread crumbs; sprinkle over potatoes. Sprinkle with paprika.
6. Bake, uncovered, for 15 to 20 minutes, until top is brown and bubbly.
Makes 4 servings

Creamed Corn

2 ounces Cream Cheese, cubed
2 Tablespoons milk
1 (14-3/4 oz.) can cream-style corn
1 (10 oz.) pkg frozen corn, thawed
1/2 cup Shredded Sharp Cheddar Cheese
1/3 cup sliced green onions

Directions

1. In medium saucepan, heat cream cheese and milk on medium heat until cream cheese is melted, stirring frequently.
2. Stir in corn; cook 4 minutes or until heated through, stirring occasionally.
3. Spoon into serving dish; sprinkle with Cheddar and onions.
Makes 6 Servings

Tip: To add a little spice, add a few drops hot sauce.

Parmesan Asparagus

1 bunch of medium sized asparagus, about 1 lb
2 Tablespoons extra virgin olive oil
2 Tablespoons freshly grated Parmesan cheese
1 freshly grated lemon rind
Salt and freshly ground black pepper

Directions

1. Thoroughly rinse asparagus, break off the tough, white bottoms and discard. Cut into 2 inch sections, slicing the asparagus at a slight diagonal.
2. Fill a medium sized saucepan half way with water, bring to a boil. Add the asparagus and reduce heat slightly to a simmer. Parboil the asparagus for exactly 2 minutes. Drain the hot water. While the asparagus are still hot, toss them in a bowl with the olive oil, Parmesan, and lemon rind. Salt and pepper to taste; Serve warm or room temperature.
Makes 4 Servings

Thai Green Bean Casserole

1 ½ pounds thin green beans
2 Tablespoons canola oil
1 pound shiitake mushrooms, discard stems, slice caps
2 shallots, thinly sliced crosswise
2 garlic cloves, thinly sliced
1 (14-oz) can unsweetened coconut milk
2 Tablespoons Thai red curry paste
1 teaspoon cornstarch mixed with 1 tablespoon of water
Kosher salt and freshly ground pepper
¾ cup roasted peanuts, chopped

Directions

1. Preheat the oven to 350 degrees F. In a steamer or large saucepan with steamer insert steam the beans until tender, about 4 minutes. Drain very well on paper towels.
2. In a large nonstick skillet, over medium heat; add 1 tablespoon of the oil heat until hot. Add the mushrooms and cook over moderate heat, turning once, until browned, about 6 minutes. Transfer to a plate.

3. In the same skillet, heat the remaining 1 tablespoon of oil. Add the shallots and cook over medium heat until lightly browned, about 4 minutes. Add the garlic and cook until fragrant, about 1 minute. Whisk in the coconut milk, red curry paste and the cornstarch mixture until smooth. Add the sauce to the skillet and cook over medium heat, stirring occasionally, until slightly thickened, about 5 minutes. Season with salt and pepper
4. In a large bowl, toss the green beans with the mushrooms. Add the sauce and toss to coat thoroughly. Transfer the beans to a shallow 3 quart baking dish and sprinkle the peanuts over the top. Bake for about 15 minutes, until heated through and the peanuts are lightly golden.
Make Ahead: This recipe can be prepared through Step 3 and refrigerated overnight. Reheat the sauce before continuing.

Cauliflower with Peas and Mushrooms

½ ounce dried shiitake mushrooms
1 small cauliflower, broken into flowerets
Vegetable cooking spray
2 teaspoons margarine
1 teaspoon vegetable oil
1 clove garlic, minced
½ cup frozen English peas
1 Tablespoon lemon juice
¼ teaspoon salt
1/8 teaspoon pepper

Directions

Pour boiling water over mushrooms to cover let stand 30 minutes or until softened. Drain well. Pat dry between paper towels; remove and discard stems. Cut mushrooms into 1-inch pieces

Arrange cauliflower in a vegetable steamer over boiling water. Cover and steam 5 minutes or until tender-crisp
Coat large nonstick skillet with cooking spray; add margarine and oil; place over medium-high heat until hot. Add garlic, sauté 2 minutes, stirring occasionally. Stir in reserved mushrooms, peas and remaining ingredients. Cook 5 minutes or until thoroughly heated. Season with salt and pepper to taste
Makes 6 Servings

Sautéed Cherry Tomatoes with Garlic and Basil

If you never thought of cooking cherry tomatoes, but sautéed, they make a colorful, tasty side dish. Both cherry and grape tomatoes can be cooked using this technique; but the grape variety is sweeter and more flavorful.

1 Tablespoon olive oil
2 pints cherry or grape tomatoes
Salt and freshly ground black pepper
2 garlic cloves, minced
1 Tablespoon minced fresh basil
1 Tablespoon extra-virgin olive oil

Directions

1. Heat olive oil in a large (12-inch) skillet over medium-high heat until it just starts to smoke. Add tomatoes and season with salt and pepper, to taste. Sauté, shaking pan frequently, until tomatoes soften and skins just start to wrinkle, about 2 minutes. Stir in garlic and continue to shake pan until garlic is fragrant.
2. Stir in basil and extra-virgin olive oil and serve.
Makes 6 servings

Chapter 5: Holiday Pies

Easy Pie Crust

Corn oil margarine is the secret to this crusts never-fail success

Single Pie Crust
1¼ cups flour, unsifted
1/8 teaspoon salt
½ cup margarine (Mazola works well), chilled
2 to 3 Tablespoons cold water

Directions

In medium bowl, combine flour and salt. With a pastry blender or 2 knives, (also works well if you use your fingers like I do) cut margarine until mixture resembles fine crumbs. Sprinkle water over mixture while tossing to blend well. Press dough firmly into a ball. On lightly floured surface roll into a 12-inch circle. Fit loosely into 9-inch pie plate. Trim and flute edge. Fill and bake according to recipe.

Classic Pecan Pie

3 eggs
1 cup sugar
1 cup light or dark corn syrup
2 Tablespoons butter, melted
1 teaspoon vanilla
1 ½ cups pecans
1 easy pie crust or 1 (9-inch) frozen deep dish pie crust

Directions

Preheat oven to 350 degrees F. In a medium bowl; beat eggs slightly. Add sugar, corn syrup, butter and vanilla; stir well until blended. Stir in pecans. Pour into pie crust.
Bake 50 to 55 minutes or until knife inserted halfway between center and edge comes out clean. Cool on wire rack
Makes 8 servings

Note: If using frozen pie crust: Do not thaw: Preheat over and a cookie sheet. Pour filling into frozen crust. Bake on cookie sheet.

Almond Amaretto Pie

3 eggs
1 cup sugar
1 cup light or dark corn syrup
2 Tablespoons butter
1 teaspoon vanilla
½ teaspoon almond extract
2 Tablespoons almond flavored liqueur
1 cup sliced almonds
1 easy pie crust or 1 (9-inch) frozen deep dish pie crust

Directions

Preheat oven to 350 degrees F. In a medium bowl; beat eggs slightly. Add sugar, corn syrup, butter and vanilla, almond extract and almond liqueur; stir well until blended. Stir in sliced almonds. Pour into pie crust.
Bake 50 to 55 minutes or until knife inserted halfway between center and edge comes out clean. Cool on wire rack
Makes 8 servings

Note: If using frozen pie crust: Do not thaw: Preheat over and a cookie sheet. Pour filling into frozen crust. Bake on cookie sheet.

Butterscotch Pecan Pie

3 eggs
1 cup sugar
1 cup light or dark corn syrup
¼ cup heavy or whipping cream
1 teaspoon vanilla
1 ½ cups pecans
1 easy pie crust or 1 (9-inch) frozen deep dish pie crust

Directions

Preheat oven to 350 degrees F. In a medium bowl; beat eggs slightly. Add sugar, corn syrup, whipping cream and vanilla; stir well until blended. Stir in pecans. Pour into pie crust.
Bake 50 to 55 minutes or until knife inserted halfway between center and edge comes out clean. Cool on wire rack
Makes 8 servings

Note: If using frozen pie crust: Do not thaw: Preheat over and a cookie sheet. Pour filling into frozen crust. Bake on cookie sheet.

Bourbon Pecan Pie

3 eggs
1 cup sugar
1 cup light or dark corn syrup
2 Tablespoons butter

1 teaspoon vanilla
2 Tablespoons Bourbon
1 ½ cups pecans
1 easy pie crust or 1 (9-inch) frozen deep dish pie crust

Directions

Preheat oven to 350 degrees F. In a medium bowl; beat eggs slightly. Add sugar, corn syrup, butter, vanilla and bourbon; stir well until blended. Stir in pecans. Pour into pie crust.
Bake 50 to 55 minutes or until knife inserted halfway between center and edge comes out clean. Cool on wire rack
Makes 8 servings

Note: If using frozen pie crust: Do not thaw: Preheat over and a cookie sheet. Pour filling into frozen crust. Bake on cookie sheet.

Pumpkin Cheese-Swirl Pie

1 (3oz) pkg. cream cheese
½ cup light corn syrup, divided
½ teaspoon vanilla
1 cup canned solid packed pumpkin
2 eggs
½ cup evaporated milk
¼ cup sugar
2 teaspoon pumpkin pie spice
¼ teaspoon salt
1 easy pie crust or 1 (9-inch) frozen deep dish pie crust

Directions

1. Preheat oven to 325 degrees F. In a small bowl with mixer at medium speed, beat cream cheese until light and fluffy. Gradually beat in ¼ cup corn syrup and vanilla until smooth; set aside.
2. In medium bowl combine pumpkin, eggs, evaporated milk, remaining ¼ cup corn syrup, sugar, pumpkin pie spice and salt. Beat until smooth. Pour into pie crust. Drop Tablespoons of cream cheese mixture onto pumpkin filling. With knife or small spatula, swirls mixture to give a marbled effect.
3. Bake 50 to 60 minutes or until knife inserted halfway between center and edge comes out clean. Cool completely on wire rack. Makes 8 Servings

Apple Brandy Praline Pie

Praline Topping (recipe follows)
¼ cup sugar
3 Tablespoons flour
¼ teaspoon salt
3 eggs
½ cup light or dark corn syrup
¼ cup butter or margarine
2 Tablespoons apple brandy or regular brandy
2 medium apples, peeled and thinly sliced
1 easy pie crust or 1 (9-inch) frozen deep dish pie crust

Directions

1. Preheat oven to 350 degrees F. **Prepare praline topping**; set aside. In a large bowl combine sugar, flour and salt. Beat in eggs, corn syrup, butter and brandy. Stir in apples. Pour into pie crust. Sprinkle with praline topping.

2. Bake 45 to 50 minutes or until puffed and set. Cool completely on wire rack.
Makes 8 Servings

Note: If using frozen pie crust: Do not thaw: Preheat over and a cookie sheet. Pour filling into frozen crust. Bake on cookie sheet.

Praline Topping

1 cup coarsely chopped pecans
¼ cup flour
¼ cup packed brown sugar
2 Tablespoons butter or margarine, softened

In a small bowl; combine pecans, flour, brown sugar and butter. Mix with a fork until crumbly.

Blueberry Pie

2 pints fresh or frozen blueberries (4 cups)
¾ cup sugar
3 Tablespoons cornstarch
3 Tablespoons water
1 teaspoon lemon rind, grated
½ teaspoon cinnamon
¼ teaspoon nutmeg
2 Tablespoons unsalted butter
1 egg, well beaten with 1 pinch salt, for egg wash
2 Tablespoons sugar, for top of pie
2 easy pie crust or 2 (9-inch) frozen deep dish pie crust

Directions

1. Combine 1 cup berries with ¾ cup sugar in saucepan. Simmer on low heat until sugar is dissolved and mixture is very liquid; about 5 minutes. In bowl combine cornstarch and water. Add to saucepan with blueberries. Cook over medium heat until mixture comes to full boil and is clear and thick. Pour hot mixture into a large bowl. Cool until just warm. Fold in remaining 3 cups of blueberries, lemon rind, cinnamon, nutmeg and butter. Let cool before filling pie crust. Add top crust and brush with egg wash, sprinkle with sugar.
2. Preheat oven to 400°F but reduce heat to 375°F when you put pie in oven. Bake about 40 minutes. Check pie halfway through baking; cover edges with a strip of foil if necessary to prevent the edges from over browning.
Makes 8 Servings

Pumpkin Pie

1 (16 ounce) can pumpkin
1 (14 ounce) sweetened condensed milk
2 eggs
1 teaspoon ground cinnamon
½ teaspoon ground ginger
½ teaspoon ground nutmeg
¼ teaspoon ground cloves
½ teaspoon salt
1 easy pie crust or 1 (9-inch) frozen deep dish pie crust

Directions

1. Preheat oven to 425 degrees F. In a large mixer bowl, combine all ingredients, except pastry shell.
2. Bake 15 minutes. Reduce oven temperature to 350 degrees F. bake 35 to 40 minutes longer or until knife inserted 1 inch from edge comes out clean. Cool. Garnish as desired. Refrigerate leftovers
Makes one 9-inch pie

Sweet Potato Pie

1 (9 inch) unbaked pie crust
2 cups cooked and mashed sweet potatoes
2 Tablespoons butter or margarine, softened
2 eggs, beaten
1 cup Granulated sugar
1 Tablespoon all-purpose flour
½ teaspoon salt
¼ teaspoon ground cinnamon
¼ teaspoon ground ginger
½ cup buttermilk
¼ teaspoon baking soda
2 teaspoon vanilla extract

Directions

1. Preheat oven to 350 degrees F.
2. Blend mashed sweet potatoes, butter or margarine, and eggs. In a separate bowl, mix sugar, flour, and salt. Mix in cinnamon and ginger. Add to sweet potato mixture and stir until well blended.
3. Mix buttermilk and baking soda. Add to sweet potato mixture and stir well. Stir in vanilla extract. Pour filling into prepared pastry shell.
4. Bake in preheated oven for 70 minutes, until the center is set.

Caramel Crunch Cheesecake

2 cups graham cracker crumbs
3 Tablespoons finely chopped peanuts
6 Tablespoons butter or margarine, melted
2 (8 oz.) pkg. cream cheese, softened
1/3 cup firmly packed brown sugar
1/4 cup corn syrup
2 Tablespoons cornstarch
3 large eggs
1/3 cup sour cream
2 teaspoons vanilla extract
6 Snickers candy bars (2.07 oz. each), coarsely chopped (about 3 cups)
¼ cup chopped peanuts
¾ cup milk chocolate chips
¼ cup plus 2 Tablespoons sour cream
1 Tablespoon firmly packed brown sugar
¼ cup whole peanuts
10 caramel candies, unwrapped

Directions

1. Preheat oven to 350 degree F. Combine graham cracker crumbs, peanuts, and melted butter in medium bowl. Press into bottom and halfway up sides of 9-inch springform pan.

2. Beat cream cheese with electric mixer at medium speed until smooth. Beat in brown sugar, corn syrup, and cornstarch. Add eggs one at a time, beating well after each addition. Stir in sour cream and vanilla. Stir in chopped candy bars and peanuts. Pour over Crust.

3. Bake 15 minutes. Reduce oven temperature to 300 degree F and bake 1- ¼ hours more or until top of cheesecake is no longer wet or glossy. Remove cake from oven; run knife around edge.

Turn oven off and return cake to oven 1 hour more. Cool completely on wire rack. Cover and refrigerate overnight.

To Make Topping:

4. Melt chocolate chips, stirring frequently, in small saucepan over low heat. Stir in ¼ cup sour cream and the brown sugar. Spread over cheesecake and sprinkle peanuts on top. Melt caramels, stirring constantly, in heavy saucepan over low heat. Remove from heat and stir in 2 Tablespoons sour cream. Drizzle over cheesecake.
Makes 16 servings

Chocolate Raspberry Cheesecake

Quick easy and delicious: Prep: 10 minutes plus refrigerating

½ cup raspberry fruit spread
1 ready-to-use graham cracker crumb crust (6-oz or 9-in)
2 (8-oz) pkgs cream cheese, softened
1 ¼ cups chocolate flavored dessert topping
1 (8-oz) Tub cool whip whipped topping, thawed

Directions

1. Spread fruit spread onto bottom of crust.
2. Mix cream cheese and dessert topping with electric mixer on medium speed until smooth. Gently stir in whipped topping.
3. Spoon over fruit spread in crust. Refrigerate 3 hours or until set. Drizzle with additional dessert topping, if desired
Makes 8 Servings

Brownie Bottom Cheesecake

1 (10 to 16-oz) pkg. brownie mix any variety (8x8-inch pan size)
3 (8-oz each) cream cheese, softened
¼ cup sugar
1 teaspoon vanilla
½ cup sour cream
3 eggs

Directions

1. Prepare and bake brownie mix as directed on package for 8x8-inch square pan; in well-greased 9-inch spring form pan.
2. Mix cream cheese, sugar and vanilla on medium speed until well blended. Blend in sour cream. Add eggs mixing on low speed just until blended. Pour over brownie crust.
3. Bake at 325 degrees F. for 60 to 65 minutes or until set if using a Silver Spring form pan. (Bake at 300 degrees F. for 60 to 65 minutes or until center is almost set if using a dark nonstick spring form pan.) Run knife or medal spatula around rim of pan to loosen cake; cool before removing rim of pan. Refrigerate 4 hours or overnight.
Makes 12 Servings

Pumpkin Marble Cheese Cake

Crust
2 cups gingersnap cookie crumbs
½ cup chopped pecans
6 Tablespoons Butter or margarine, melted

Filling

3 (8-oz) pkgs Cream Cheese, softened
1 cup sugar, divided
1 teaspoon vanilla
3 eggs
1 cup canned pumpkin
1 teaspoon ground cinnamon
¼ teaspoon ground nutmeg
Dash ground cloves

Directions

Crust
Mix crumbs, pecans and butter, press onto the bottom and 2-inches up side of 9-inch springform pan.

Filling
1. Mix cream cheese, ¼ cup sugar and vanilla with electric mixer on medium speed until well blended. Add eggs, mixing on low speed just until blended. Reserve 1½ cups batter: Add remaining ¼ cup sugar, pumpkin and spices to remaining batter; mix well. Spoon ½ the pumpkin batter and spices to remaining batter, mix well. Spoon ½ of the pumpkin batter over crust; top with spoonfuls of plain batter. Repeat layers. Cut through batter with knife several times for marble effect

2. Bake at 325 degrees F. for 55 minutes or until center is almost set if using a Silver Spring form pan. (If using a dark nonstick springform pan Bake at 300 degrees F. for 55 minutes or until center is almost set.) Run knife or metal spatula around rim of pan to loosen cake; cool before removing rim of pan. Refrigerate 4 hours or overnight.

Chapter 6: Bars and Cookies

When the occasion calls for a bite-size dessert, bar cookies are the favorite. Enjoy some of our favorites.

Holiday Cheese Cake Bars

1 ½ cups graham cracker crumbs
1/3 cup butter or margarine, melted
3 Tablespoons sugar
3 (8-oz) Cream Cheese, softened
¾ cup sugar
1 teaspoon vanilla
3 eggs

Directions

1. Mix crumbs, butter and 3 Tablespoons sugar; press onto bottom of 13x9-inch baking pan
2. Mix cream cheese, ¾ cup sugar and vanilla with electric mixer at medium speed until well blended. Add egg, mix until blended. Pour over crust.
3. Bake at 350 degrees F. for 30 minutes or until center is almost set. Cool. Refrigerate 3 hours or overnight. Cut bars. Decorate bars with decorating gels and sprinkles to resemble gifts. Store left over bars in the refrigerator.
Makes 24 Bars

Snowmen Cookies

1 (8-oz) pkg. Cream Cheese, softened
1 cup powdered sugar
¾ cup (1 ½ sticks) Butter or margarine
1 teaspoon vanilla
2 ½ cups flour
½ teaspoon baking soda

Sifted powdered sugar
Miniature peanut butter cups (optional)

Directions

1. Mix cream cheese, 1 cup powdered sugar, butter and vanilla with an electric mixer on medium speed until well blended. Add flour and baking soda; mix well.
2. Shape dough into equal number of ½-inch and 1-inch diameter balls. Using 1 small and 1 large ball for each snowman, place balls, slightly overlapping, on ungreased cookie sheets. Flatten to ¼-inch thickness with bottom of glass dipped in additional flour. Repeat with remaining balls.
3. Bake at 325 degrees F. for 19 to 21 minutes or until light golden brown. Cool on wire racks. Sprinkle each snowman with sifted powdered sugar. Decorate with icing as desired. Cut peanut butter cups in half for hats.
Makes about 3 dozen

Shortbread cookies

1 ½ cups (3 sticks) butter or margarine, softened
1 (8-oz) pkg. Cream Cheese, softened
½ cup granulated sugar
3 cups flour
Powdered sugar

Directions

1. Mix butter, cream cheese and sugar until well blended. Mix in flour.
2. Shape dough into 1-inch balls; place on ungreased cookie sheets.

3. Bake at 400 degrees F. for 10 to 13 minutes or until light golden brown and set; cool on wire racks. Sprinkle with powdered sugar

Frosted Pumpkin Squares

Cake
¾ cup (1½ sticks) butter or margarine
2 cups granulated sugar
1 (16-oz) can pumpkin puree
4 eggs
2 cups flour
2 teaspoons baking powder
1 teaspoon ground cinnamon
½ teaspoon baking powder
½ teaspoon salt
¼ teaspoon ground nutmeg
1 cup chopped walnuts

Frosting
1 (8-oz) Cream Cheese, softened
1/3 cup butter or margarine
1 teaspoon vanilla
3 cups sifted powdered sugar

Directions

Cake:
1. Mix butter and sugar with electric mixer on medium speed until light and fluffy. Blend in pumpkin and eggs. Mix in combined dry ingredients. Stir in walnuts.
2. Spread into greased 15x10x1-inch baking pan
3. Bake at 350 degrees F. for 30 to 35 minutes or until toothpick inserted in center comes out clean; cool

Frosting
Mix: Cream cheese, butter and vanilla in large bowl with electric mixer until creamy. Gradually add sugar, mixing well after each addition. Spread on cake. Cut into squares.
Makes 24 Bars

Creamy Lemon Bars

1 pkg. (2layer size) Lemon cake mix
3 large eggs, divided
½ cup oil
2 (8-oz) pkg. cream cheese, softened
1 (8-oz) container Sour cream
½ cup sugar
1 teaspoon grated lemon peel
1 Tablespoon Lemon juice
Powdered sugar

Directions

1. Mix cake mix, 1 egg and oil. Press mixture onto bottom and up sides of lightly greased 15x10x1-inch baking pan. Bake at 350 degrees F for 10 minutes.
2. Mix cream cheese with electric mixer on medium speed until smooth. Add remaining 2 eggs, sour cream, sugar, lemon peel and juice; mix until blended. Pour batter over crust.
3. Bake at 350 degrees F. for 30 to 35 minutes or until filling is just set in center and edges are light golden brown. Cool. Sprinkle with powdered sugar. Cut into bars. Store leftover bars in refrigerator
Makes 24 Bars.

Sugar Cookies

1 (8-oz) pkg. Cream Cheese, Softened
1 cup (2 sticks) butter or margarine, softened
2/3 cup sugar
½ teaspoon vanilla
2 cups flour
Colored sugar, sprinkles and colored gels

Directions

1. Mix cream cheese, butter, 2/3 cup sugar and vanilla with electric mixer on medium speed until well blended. Mix in flour, Refrigerate several hours or overnight.
2. Roll dough to ¼-inch thickness on lightly floured surface. Cut into desired shape; sprinkle with colored sugar. Place on ungreased cookie sheets.
3. Bake at 350 degrees F. for 12 to 15 minutes or until edges are lightly browned. Cool on wire racks. Decorate as desired with colored sugar. Sprinkles and colored gels:
Makes about 3 ½ dozen

Pecan Pie Bars

Bar Cookie (recipe below)
2 eggs
¾ cup Light or Dark corn syrup
¾ cup sugar
2 Tablespoons butter or margarine, melted
1 teaspoon vanilla
1 ¼ cups coarsely chopped pecans

Directions

Preheat oven to 350 degrees F. prepare bar cookie crust. Meanwhile, in large bowl beat eggs, corn syrup, sugar, butter and vanilla until well blended. Stir in pecans. Pour over hot crust; spread evenly.
Bake 20 minutes or until filling is firm around edges and slightly firm in center. Cool completely on wire rack. Cut into 2 x 1½ -inch bars.
Makes about 32 bars

Bar Cookie Crust

You will need this recipe for the some of the following recipes.

Nonstick corn oil spray
2 cups flour
½ cup (1 stick) cold margarine or butter, cut into; pieces
1/3 cup sugar
¼ teaspoon salt

Directions

Preheat oven to 350 degrees F. Spray 13x9-inch baking pan with cooking spray. In large bowl with mixer at medium speed, beat flour, margarine, sugar and salt until mixture resembles coarse crumbs. Press firmly into bottom and ¼ -inch up sides of prepared pan.
Bake 15 minutes or until golden brown. Top with desired filling, Complete as recipe directs.

Almond Toffee Triangles

Sliced almonds in a rich, toffee-like candy filling make an elegant tiny dessert.

1 recipe <u>Bar Cookie Mix</u> (above)
1/3 cup light or dark corn syrup
1/3 cup packed brown sugar
3 Tablespoon margarine or butter
¼ cup heavy whipping cream
1 ½ cups sliced almonds
1 teaspoon vanilla

Directions

1. Preheat oven to 350 degrees F. Prepare Bar Cookie Crust.
2. Meanwhile, in medium saucepan combine corn syrup, brown sugar, margarine and cream. Bring to a boil over medium heat; remove from heat. Stir in almonds and vanilla. Pour over hot crust; spread evenly.
3. Bake 12 minutes or until set and golden. Cool completely on wire rack. Cut into 2-inch squares; cut diagonally in half for triangles.
Makes 48 Triangles

Chocolate Chip Walnut Bars

This holiday cookie is a year-round favorite

1 recipe <u>Bar cookie crust</u>
2 eggs
½ cup light or dark corm syrup
½ cup sugar
2 Tablespoons margarine or butter
1 cup (6-oz) semisweet chocolate chips
¼ cup chopped walnuts

Directions

1. Preheat oven to 350 degrees F. Prepare Bar cookie Crust. Meanwhile, in medium bowl, beat eggs, corn syrup, sugar and margarine until well blended. Stir in chocolate chips and walnuts. Pour over hot crust; spread evenly.

2. Bake 15 to 18 minutes or until set. Cool completely on wire rack. Cut into 2 x 1 ½ -inch bars.
Makes 24 Bars

Cranberry Walnut Bars

Look for dried cranberries in supermarkets or gourmet stores.

1 recipe Bar Cookie Crust
2 eggs
½ cup light or dark corn syrup
½ cup sugar
2 Tablespoons margarine or butter, melted
1 cup dried cranberries or raisins (about 6-oz)
¾ cup chopped walnuts

Directions
Preheat oven to 350 degrees F. Prepare Bar cookie crust. Meanwhile, in medium bowl beat eggs, corn syrup, sugar and margarine until well blended. Stir in cranberries and walnuts. Pour over hot crust; spread evenly.

Bake 15 to 20 minutes or until set. Cool completely on wire rack. Cut into 2x1 ½ -inch bars.
Makes about 32 bars

Cherry Nut Thumbprints

Rich shortbread cookies, coated with chopped walnuts and filled with cherry pie filling are as delicious as they are also pretty

1 cup (2 sticks) margarine or butter
½ cup sugar
1 teaspoon vanilla
½ cup light corn syrup
2 eggs, separated
2 ½ cups flour
¼ teaspoon salt
2 cups finely chopped walnuts
1 (21-oz) can cherry pie filling

Directions

In a large bowl with an electric mixer at medium speed, beat margarine, sugar and vanilla until smooth. Beat in corn syrup and egg yolks. Stir in flour and salt until blended. Cover; chill 1 hour or until dough is firm:
In small bowl lightly beat egg whites. Roll dough into 1-inch balls; dip in egg whites and roll in walnuts. Place 2 Inches apart on greased cookie sheets. With thumb make indentation in center of each cookie. Chill 30 minutes
Preheat oven to 325 degrees F. Bake 20 to 35 minutes or until golden. Remove to wire rack. Cool completely. Fill with cherry pie filling.
Makes about 4 dozen cookies

Chocolate Peppermint Cookies

A glass of cold milk and freshly baked chocolate peppermint cookies makes an unbeatable afternoon snack.

½ cup margarine, or butter, softened

½ cup sugar
½ cup firmly packed brown sugar
½ cup frozen egg substitute, thawed
1 teaspoon vanilla extract
2 ¼ cups all-purpose flour
1 teaspoon baking powder
¼ teaspoon baking soda
¼ teaspoon salt
¼ cup plus 1 Tablespoon unsweetened cocoa
2/3 cup finely crushed peppermint candies (about 30 candies)
Vegetable cooking spray

Directions

1. Beat margarine with an electric mixer at medium speed until creamy; gradually add white and brown sugars, beating well. Add egg substitute and vanilla; beat well.
2. Combine flour, baking powder, baking soda, salt and cocoa. Add to margarine mixture, stirring until just blended. Stir in crushed candy. Drop dough by level Tablespoonful's, 2-inches apart, on cookie sheets sprayed with vegetable spray.
3. Bake at 350 degrees F for 10 to 12 minutes. Remove from cookie sheets, let cool on wire racks
Makes 44 cookies

Granola Meringue Cookies

Store these sweet treats in an air tight container to keep then crisp.

3 egg whites
½ teaspoon cream of tartar
¼ cup plus 2 Tablespoons sugar
¾ cup granola cereal without raisins
¼ teaspoon vanilla extract

¼ teaspoon almond extract

Directions

1. Line 2 baking sheets with parchment paper; set aside
2. Beat eggs whites and cream of tartar; with an electric mixer on high speed until foamy. Gradually add sugar, 1 Tablespoon at a time, beating until stiff peaks form and sugar dissolves (2 to 4 minutes) Fold in cereal, vanilla and almond extracts.
3. Drop mixture by level Tablespoonful 2 inches apart onto prepared baking sheets. Bake at 225 degrees F. for 1 hour and 10 minutes. Turn oven off. Cool in oven for 2 hours with the oven door closed. Carefully remove cookies from paper; let cool completely on wire racks.
Makes 4 dozen cookies

Fudgy Mint Brownies

¼ cup margarine, softened
2/3 cup sugar
2 egg whites, divided
2 Tablespoon water
2 teaspoons vanilla extract
¾ cup all-purpose flour
¼ teaspoon baking powder
1/3 cup unsweetened cocoa
8 peppermint candy pieces, finely crushed
Vegetable cooking spray

Directions

1. Beat margarine with an electric mixer at medium speed until creamy; gradually add sugar, beating well. Add egg whites, water and vanilla; beat well.
2. Combine flour, baking powder, cocoa and candy; add to margarine mixture, stirring just until dry ingredients are moistened; set aside.
3. Pour into an 8-in square pan coated with vegetable spray. Bake: at 350 degrees F. for 22 to 24 minutes or until edges pull away from pan slightly. Cool in pan on a wire rack.
Makes 16 Brownies

Persimmon cookies

2 large ripe persimmons, peeled and coarsely chopped
1 cup sugar
2/3 cup vegetable oil
1 large egg
2 cups all-purpose flour
1 teaspoon baking soda
1 teaspoon ground cinnamon
1 cup raisins
1 cup chopped walnuts
1 cup sifted powdered sugar
3 Tablespoons lemon juice

Directions

1. Preheat oven to 375 degrees F. Lightly grease cookie sheets.
2. Position knife blade in food processor bowl; add persimmon, and process until smooth, stopping once to scrape down sides. Measure 1 cup pulp
3. Combine pulp, sugar, oil and egg, stirring until smooth.

4. In a large bowl, combine flour, soda and cinnamon; add persimmon mixture, stirring until blended. Stir in raisins and walnuts.
5. Drop dough by rounded teaspoonful's onto lightly greased cookie sheets.
6. Bake in preheated oven for 9 minutes. Transfer to wire racks placed on wax paper.
7. Combine powdered sugar and lemon juice, stir until smooth; drizzle over warm cookies. Cool
Makes 5 dozen

Chapter 7: Breads and Rolls

Pandoro

This classic Italian bread is traditionally baked in a tall, star- pan. If you can't find one, use an 8-inch springform pan instead. "Sponge" takes on a new meaning in this recipe; it's a yeast mixture used like a starter for this bread

'Sponge" recipe below
1 teaspoon active dry yeast
1 Tablespoon warm water (105 to 115 degrees F)
6 ½ cups bread flour, divided
¼ cup sugar
2 large eggs
¼ cup butter, softened and cut into pieces
4 large eggs
2 egg yolks
1 cup sugar
1 teaspoon salt
2 teaspoon vanilla extract
1 ½ Tablespoons grated lemon rind
1 ¼ cups butter or margarine, softened and cut into pieces
½ cup chopped candied citron
¼ to ½ cups bread flour
Butter-flavored cooking spray

Directions

1. Prepare "sponge" according to recipe, and set aside.
2. Combine yeast and warm water in a 1-cup liquid measuring cup; let stand 5 minutes. Stir yeast mixture, 2½ cups flour, ¼ cup sugar, and 2 eggs into "sponge"; stir vigorously with a wooden spoon until blended. Gradually stir in ¼ cup butter. Cover and let

rise in a warm place (85 degrees f.). Free from drafts. 45 minutes or until dough has doubled in size:

3. Add 4 eggs and next 5 ingredients; beat at medium speed with electric mixer until smooth. Gradually add 2 cups flour, beating until blended. Stir in remaining 2 cups of flour with a wooden spoon. Gradually stir in 1 ¼ cups butter and citron.

4. Turn dough out onto a heavily floured surface, and knead until smooth and elastic (about 5 minutes), adding an additional ¼ to ½ cup bread flour, if needed. Place in a well-greased bowl, turning to grease top. Cover and let rise in a warm place 1 ½ hours or until doubled in size.

5. Punch dough down, and divide in half; place in two pandoro pans or 8-inch springform pans coated with cooking spray. Cover and let rise in a warm place (85 degrees F.) Free from drafts, for 1½ hours or until doubled in size. Bake at 350 degrees F. for 30 minutes. Cover with foil, and reduce heat to 300 degrees F.; bake an additional 20 minutes.

Makes 2 loaves

"Sponge"

2 packages active dry yeast
½ cup warm water (105 to 115 degrees F)
1 large egg
2 Tablespoons sugar
¾ cup bread flour

Directions

Combine yeast and warm water in a 1-cup measuring cup; let stand 5 minutes. Combine yeast mixture and remaining ingredients in a large mixing bowl; beat at medium speed with an electric mixer until mixture is smooth. Cover "Sponge" and let rise in a warm place (85 degrees F) free from drafts, 30 minutes or until doubled in size.

Makes 1 ½ cups

Parmesan Bread Twists

These bread twists are better than Olive Garden

Dough:
1½ teaspoon yeast
5 Tablespoon plus 1 teaspoon sugar
1 egg, room temperature
3 Tablespoons butter
¼ cup milk
½ teaspoon salt
2 – 2½ cups flour

Toppings:
2 ounces unsalted butter
½ teaspoon garlic salt
½ cup grated parmesan cheese
Additional butter to brush breadsticks after baking

Directions

1. Mix yeast and 1 teaspoon sugar in ¼ cup warm water. Let stand 5 minutes. Combine milk, 5 tablespoons sugar, and butter and microwave on 50% power (I use defrost) for 2 minutes or until butter is almost melted. Stir. Combine yeast mixture, milk mixture, and egg. While mixing, gradually add 2 cups flour and salt. Add additional flour until smooth dough forms. Place dough in oiled bowl, and turn dough o coat. Cover with plastic wrap. Rise for 20-30 minutes or until double in size.
2. Preheat oven to 375°F. Melt cube of butter in large baking sheet with 1-inch sides. Remove from oven. Roll out dough on greased surface to ¼-inch thickness. Cut into 1-inch strips. Fold each strip in half and twist. Roll each twist in butter and place 2 inches apart on baking sheet. Sprinkle with garlic salt and parmesan cheese. Cover with plastic wrap and let rise for 30

minutes. Bake at 375 degrees F. for 12-15 minutes or until golden. Immediately brush with additional melted butter.

French Honey-Spice Bread

1 Tablespoon butter to grease pan
1 ½ cups (350ml) honey
2 Tablespoons dark brown sugar
¾ cup plus 2 Tbsp. (125g) whole-wheat flour
¾ cup plus 2 Tbsp. (125g) rye flour
2 teaspoons baking powder
½ teaspoon ground cinnamon
½ teaspoon ground anise seeds
¼ teaspoon star anise, grated
¼ teaspoon ground nutmeg
¼ teaspoon ground ginger
¼ teaspoon ground cloves
Zest of 1 orange grated
2 eggs, beaten
1/3 cup plus 2 Tbsp. (100ml) milk

Directions

1. **Preheat** oven to 425 degrees F. (220C) Grease a 9 x 5 x 3in (22x12x7cm) loaf pan with oil and line the sides and bottom with waxed paper. Place the honey and sugar in a saucepan over low heat and stir until, sticky and thickened about 3 minutes.
2. **Sift** the flours, baking powder, spices and orange zest in a large bowl. Make a well in the center and pour in the eggs and milk.
3. **Stir** in the honey mixture, drawing in the flour to form a smooth batter. Pour the batter into the pan; it will be ¾ full.
4. **Bake** in the preheated oven for 1¼ hours, until dark and fragrant. Because of the high sugar content, the loaf may have

to be covered with foil to prevent it from burning, since the top will be very dark during cooling. The bread is ready when a toothpick inserted into the center comes out clean. Turn out of the loaf pan, and cool on a wire rack.

Country Oatmeal Bread

2 to 2 ¼ cups all-purpose or unbleached flour
1 cup water, heated to 105 to115 degrees F
1 pkg active yeast
2 Tablespoons nonfat instant dry milk
2 Tablespoons honey
1 Tablespoon butter, melted
1 teaspoon salt
1 cup rolled oats
Topping
1 egg, beaten
2 Tablespoons sunflower seeds (shelled)

Directions

1. Lightly spoon flour into measuring cup; level off. In a large bowl combine water, yeast, dry milk and honey. Let stand for 5 minutes. Add butter, salt and rolled oats; stir in 2 cups of flour until dough pulls cleanly away from the sides of the bowl. On a floured surface, knead in up to ¼ cup of flour until dough is smooth and elastic, about 5 minutes. Turn dough into in to a greased bowl; shape into a ball and turn to grease all sides. Cover loosely with a towel. Let rise in a warm place (80 to 85 degrees F.) until doubled in size, about 45 to 60 minutes.
2. Grease cookie sheet. Punch down dough several times to remove all air bubbles. Shape into a smooth ball; place on

greased cookie sheet. Flatten ball to 6-inch diameter. Cover loosely with a towel. Let rise in a warm place until doubled in size, 45 to 60 minutes.

3. Preheat oven to 375 degrees F. Uncover dough. Brush with beaten egg, sprinkle with sunflower seeds. Bake for 15 to 30 minutes or until loaf sounds hollow when lightly tapped.
Makes 1 (12 slice) loaf

Pumpernickel Brie Wreath

This spectacular bread makes a great centerpiece for a buffet or brunch.

1 pkg. hot roll mix
¾ cup Rye flour
2 Tablespoons unsweetened cocoa
1 Tablespoon caraway seed
1¼ cups water, heated to 120 to 130 F.
¼ cup dark molasses
2 Tablespoons butter or margarine, melted
1 egg, separated
1 Tablespoon water
Cheese
1 (8 oz) round Brie cheese
¼ cup slices or slivered almonds

Directions

1. **Grease** cookie sheet. Grease outside of 10-oz custard cup; place upside down in the center of cookie sheet. In a large bowl, combine flour mixture with yeast from foil packet, rye flour, cocoa and caraway seed. Stir in hot water, molasses, butter and egg yolk until dough pulls away from sides of bowl.

2. **Turn** dough out onto lightly floured surface. With greased or lightly floured hands, shape dough into a ball. Knead dough for 5 minutes, or until smooth, adding more flour if necessary to reduce slickness. Cover dough with large bowl; let rise 5 minutes.

3. **On** lightly floured surface, divide dough into thirds. Roll each piece into 25-inch rope. Braid ropes loosely from center to each end. Arrange braid around the custard cup on greased cookie sheet, joining ends to form a ring; pinch to seal. Cover loosely with plastic wrap and cloth towel. Let rise in a warm place (80 – 85 F.)Until almost doubled in size. 45-60 minutes.

4. **Preheat** oven to 350 degrees F. Uncover dough. In a small bowl, beat egg white with 1 Tablespoon water; Brush over braid, reserving remaining to brush on brie. Bake for 20 to 30 minutes or until bread sounds hollow when lightly tapped. Carefully loosen and remove bread from cookie sheet, cool slightly on wire rack.

5. **Before** serving, heat broiler. Brush the top of brie with remaining egg white mixture and sprinkle almonds in top. Place brie on ungreased cookie sheet; broil 4 to 6 inches from heat for 30 to 60 seconds or until almonds are toasted. Place warm bread on large round serving platter or in a basket. Cut small sections of bread into slices. Fit cheese in center; set slices back in place. Makes 1 loaf; 18 Servings

Easy Dinner Rolls

2 ½ teaspoons dry yeast
1 cup (250ml) milk
4 Tablespoons butter, melted
2 Tablespoons sugar
2 eggs, beaten
4 cups (560g) unbleached flour

2 teaspoons salt

2 Tablespoons melted butter to glaze, plus extra to grease bowl and baking sheet

Directions

1. **Sprinkle** the yeast into ½ cup (125ml) of milk in a bowl. Leave 5 minutes; stir to dissolve. Warm the remaining milk in a saucepan with the butter and sugar. Stir until butter has melted. Cool until lukewarm, and then beat in the eggs until evenly blended.

2. **Mix** the flour and salt in a large bowl. Make a well in the center and pour in the dissolved yeast and butter mixture. Mix the flour to form soft sticky dough.

3. **Turn** the dough out onto a floured surface. Knead until smooth, shiny, and elastic, about 10 minutes. Kneed in extra flour; 1 Tablespoon at a time, if dough is too sticky. Resist adding too much flour, as dough should not be dry, but soft.

4. **Place** the dough in a buttered bowl. Let rise until doubled in size, 1-1 ½ hours. Punch down, let rest for 10 minutes.

5. **Divide** the dough into two pieces. Roll out each piece to form an 8in x 16in (20cm x 40cm) rectangle. Cut each rectangle lengthwise into four strips each 2in (5cm) wide. Cut each strip into four rectangles, each 4in (10cm) long. Brush ½ of each rectangle with melted butter, and then fold in half, leaving a ½ in (1cm) flap.

6. **Place** the rolls on a buttered baking sheet so each roll overlaps slightly with the one next to it; cover with a dish towel. Proof until doubled in size, about 10 minutes.

7. **Brush** the tops of the rolls with melted butter. Bake in preheated oven 425 degrees F (220 C) for 15 to 20 minutes. Until golden and hollow sounding when tapped underneath. Cool on wire rack.

Almond-Anise Biscotti

½ cup butter or margarine
¼ cup canola or vegetable oil
1 ¼ cups sugar
6 large eggs
1 teaspoon anise oil
1 ½ teaspoons vanilla
6 to 7 cups all-purpose flour, divided
1 teaspoon baking powder
2 cups whole blanched almonds
1 ½ cups sifted powdered sugar
2 Tablespoons milk
Chopped almonds or sugar, if desired

Directions

1. Beat butter, oil and sugar with an electric mixer at medium speed until well blended. Add eggs, one at a time, beating after each addition. Stir in anise oil and vanilla.
2. Combine 6 cups flour and baking powder; add butter mixture. Gradually add enough remaining flour to make stiff dough. Stir in almonds, lightly flour hands, and divide dough into 5 portions. Shape each portion into 8-inch long log, and place on lightly greased cookie sheet; Bake at 350 degrees F. for 35 minutes or until lightly browned; cool on wire rack
3. Using a serrated knife carefully cut each log crosswise into ½ - inch slices. Place on ungreased cookie sheet; bake at 350 degrees F. for 10 minutes on each side. Cool on wire racks

4. Combine powdered sugar and milk; spread over top of each biscotti, and sprinkle with chopped almonds or sugar, if desired
Makes about 5 ½ dozen

Cinnamon Twists

4 - 4 1/3 cups all-purpose flour
1 pkg. Active dry yeast
1 cup milk
1/3 cup Butter or Margarine
1/3 cup Sugar
2 ½ teaspoons cinnamon
½ teaspoon salt
2 eggs
Glaze:
1 cup powdered sugar
¼ teaspoon milk
1 Tablespoon milk

Directions

1. Combine 2 cups flour with yeast.
2. Heat and stir milk, butter or margarine, sugar and salt until warm and butter is almost melted.
3. Add this to the flour mixture, add the eggs.
4. Beat with an electric mixer on low speed for 30 seconds, scraping the bowl, then beat on high speed for approx. 3 minutes. Stir in as much of the remaining flour (2 to 2 1/3 cups) as you can; scraping sides.
5. Turn out onto a lightly floured surface. Knead in enough remaining flour to make a smooth and elastic (about 3 - 5 minutes). Shape into a ball. Place in a lightly greased bowl. Cover and let rise in a warm place till double in size. (About 1 hour)

6. Punch dough down. Divide in half. Cover and let rest 10 minutes.

7. Roll each half of the dough into a 12 x 8 inch rectangle. Melt 3 tablespoons butter or margarine; brush half over the dough. Combine ¾ cup sugar and 2 ½ teaspoons ground cinnamon; sprinkle half of the mixture over dough. Fold dough in half and then in half again, repeat with second dough. Cut strips of dough along the short end and twist sealing the seams.

8. Place in a baking sheet. Cover; let rise till nearly double about 30 minutes.

9. Bake in a 375 degree oven for 20 to 25 minutes. (Be sure to check them, they brown easily.)

For the sugar glaze combine 1 cup sifted powdered sugar with ¼ teaspoon vanilla and 1 Tablespoon milk. Continue to add milk 1 teaspoon at a time until you get a drizzling consistency.

Orange-Cranberry Bread

This recipe is so delicious, fluffy and yummy, also makes a great gift from your kitchen. If you prefer use orange juice instead of the Grand Marnier its will still be just as yummy.

1½ cups unsalted butter, softened: plus extra to butter pans.
1½ cups sugar
4 eggs
1 cup orange juice
1 cup sour cream
2 Tablespoons freshly grated orange zest
2 teaspoons vanilla extract
4 cups all-purpose flour
1 Tablespoon baking powder
½ teaspoon salt
1½ cups dried cranberries
2 cups powdered sugar

8 Tablespoons Grand Marnier or other orange liqueur

Directions

1. Preheat oven to 350 degrees F. Butter two 9 x 5-inch loaf pans (or if making the mini loaves, butter six mini loaf pans).
2. With an electric mixer, cream butter and sugar together, on medium speed until pale and fluffy, about 3 minutes. Add eggs one at a time, mixing well after each. Add orange juice, sour cream, orange zest, and vanilla; mix until blended.
3. In a separate bowl, whisk together flour, baking powder, and salt. Add flour mixture and cranberries to butter mixture and mix just until dry ingredients are just moistened; do not over mix.
4. Pour batter into prepared loaf pans. Bake for 70 to 75 minutes for large loaves and 60 minutes for mini loaves, or until toothpick inserted in center comes out clean.
5. In a small bowl, combine powdered sugar and 7 Tablespoons Grand Marnier. Glaze should have consistency of thick maple syrup or corn syrup. If it is too thick, add additional Tablespoon liqueur.
6. Let loaves cool in pans for 10 minutes, then remove and transfer to wire rack set over a large baking sheet. With a thin skewer or long toothpick, poke deep holes in tops of loaves. Drizzle with Grand Marnier glaze so that it coats the top, runs down the sides, and seeps through the holes.
7. Let loaves cool completely, then slice and serve, or wrap and freeze.
Makes two loaves (9x5-inch)

Make Ahead Recipe:
Make loaves up to 1 month ahead and freeze. Bake and glaze loaves and allow them to cool completely. Wrap tightly with plastic wrap, put in reasealable plastic bags, and freeze. When

ready to serve, remove from freezer and defrost at room temperature.

Chapter 8: Holiday Desserts and Cakes

Cantaloupe-Champagne Sorbet

3 ½ cups chopped cantaloupe
½ cup sugar
2/3 cup champagne
2 teaspoons grated lemon rind

Directions

1. Position knife blade in food processor bowl; add all ingredients. Process until smooth: Pour mixture into an 8-inch square pan. Cover; freeze until firm.
2. Remove from freezer, and let stand 5 minutes. Break cantaloupe mixture into chunks using a fork, place in a medium bowl. Beat cantaloupe mixture with an electric mixer at medium speed until smooth. Return mixture to pan. Cover and freeze at least 2 hours. Scoop sorbet into individual dessert bowls. Serve Immediately.
Makes 4 cups

Refreshing Lime Sherbet

¼ cup plain nonfat yogurt
¼ cup nonfat cottage cheese
1 ½ cups sugar
3 ½ cups water
1 teaspoon grated lime rind

½ cup fresh lime juice
1 drop green food coloring (optional)
Lime wedges (optional)
Edible flowers (optional)

Directions

1. Combine yogurt and cottage cheese in container of a blender; cover and process until smooth, set aside.
2. In a sauce pan combine sugar, 3 ½ cups water and grated lime rind; bring to a boil. Cover; reduce heat and simmer 10 minutes. Remove from heat, stir in lime juice. Let mixture cool to room temperature
3. Combine yogurt mixture and lime mixture in a bowl, stirring well. Stir in green food coloring, if desired. Pour lime mixture into freezer can of a 2-quart hand turned or electric freezer. Freeze according to manufacturer's instructions. Pack freeze with additional ice and rock salt, and let stand for 1 hour before serving. Scoop sherbet into individual dessert bowls, if desired, garnish with lime wedges and edible flowers, if desired. Serve immediately.
Makes 5 cups

Frozen Pumpkin Dessert

¾ cup graham cracker crumbs
¼ cup sugar
3 Tablespoons margarine or butter, melted
Vegetable cooking spray
1 ½ cups canned pumpkin
¾ cup sifted powdered sugar
1 teaspoon ground cinnamon
¼ teaspoon ground cloves
¼ teaspoon ground nutmeg

¼ teaspoon salt
4 cups nonfat frozen dessert, softened
2 Tablespoons graham cracker crumbs

Directions

1. Combine first 3 ingredients, stirring well. Press mixture into bottom of an 11x7x1 ½ -inch baking dish coated with cooking spray. Bake at 350 degrees F. for 8 minutes. Let cool completely on wire rack.
2. Combine pumpkin, powdered sugar, cinnamon, cloves, nutmeg and salt in a large bowl; Stirring well. Add frozen dessert, with an electric mixer; beat on low speed for 1 minute or until smooth.
3. Spoon into prepared dish. Sprinkle 2 Tablespoons graham cracker crumbs over pumpkin mixture. Cover and freeze until firm.
Makes 10 servings

Tropical Frozen Yogurt

2 cups fresh strawberry halves
2 cups peeled, slices bananas
¼ cup sugar
¾ cup frozen pineapple juice concentrate, thawed (undiluted)
½ cup plain low-fat yogurt

Directions

1. Position knife in food processor bowl; add first 4 ingredients. Process until smooth; scrap sides of processor bowl once. Add yogurt, and pulse 3 or 4 times or until combined.

2. Pour mixture into freezer can of a 2-quart hand turned or electric freezer. Freeze according to manufacturer's instructions. Pack freezer with additional ice and rock salt, let stand 1 hour. Scoop frozen yogurt into individual dessert bowls. Serve immediately
Makes 5 ½ cups

Mango-Pineapple Sorbet

1 medium banana
1 cup mango cubes
1 cup fresh pineapple chunks
2 tablespoons water
1 tablespoon fresh lemon juice

Directions

1. Peel banana and cut into 1-in. pieces. Place banana slices, mango cubes and pineapple chunks on a wax paper-lined rimmed baking sheet. Freeze 1½ to 2 hours until completely frozen.
2. In a food processor Process fruit, water and lemon juice until smooth. Serve immediately or can be frozen up to 2 weeks.

Pumpkin Mousse

Whipped cream and spiced pumpkin mousse creates a festive dessert for the holiday season.

5 large egg yolks
1 cup sugar, divided
3 ½ cup heavy cream, divided
1 (15 ounce) canned pumpkin

2 teaspoons vanilla extract
1 ½ teaspoons ground cinnamon
½ teaspoon ground ginger
¼ teaspoon ground nutmeg
¼ teaspoon salt
2 tablespoons dark rum
1 teaspoon powdered gelatin
3 ounces shaved dark chocolate

Directions

1. Fill a large bowl halfway with ice water and set aside.
2. Whisk the yolks, ¾ cup plus 2 tablespoons sugar, and 3/4 cup cream in a medium saucepan. Heat while stirring continuously with a spatula or wooden spoon over medium-low heat, until thickened and the mixture coats the spatula or spoon, about 10 minutes. Transfer to a medium bowl and set over the ice bath. Stir to cool.
3. Add pumpkin, vanilla, spices, and salt to the egg mixture. Stir 1 tablespoon rum and 1 teaspoon gelatin together in a small bowl. Heat the remaining Tablespoon rum, and stir in to the gelatin mixture until dissolved. Gently whisk into the pumpkin mixture. Beat ½ cup cream to stiff peaks, and fold into pumpkin mixture. Pour into a shallow dish, cover and chill until cold and thick enough to fall from a spoon in heavy dollops -- about 8 hours or up to overnight.
4. Beat the remaining cream and sugar to stiff peaks. Alternately layer the pumpkin mousse and whipped cream in a glass serving dish. Sprinkle the chocolate shavings between top two layers. Serve chilled.
Makes 14 Servings

Sweet Roll Pudding

1 (7-oz) can refrigerated cinnamon raisin rolls
2 large eggs
1½ cups milk
¾ cup sugar
1 teaspoon vanilla extract
¼ cup butter
2 Tablespoons honey

Directions

1. Bake rolls according to package directions; cool and crumble. Sprinkle 3 cups crumbs into lightly greased 1½ -quart baking dish.
2. Combine eggs and milk; stir in eggs and vanilla, and pour over crumbs.
3. Combine butter and honey; pour over egg mixture.
4. Bake at 300 degrees F. for 1 hour or until golden.
Makes 4 to 6 Servings

Steamed Holiday Pudding

Steamed puddings are a long standing holiday tradition, if you have never made on I have a couple for you. Even through many ingredients are used these puddings they are simple to prepare. You will get better results if a steamed pudding mold with a locking top is used... However you can use heat-proof bowls, covered with a double thickness of buttered aluminum foil secured with string.

2 1/3 cups all-purpose flour
1 1/3 cups finely chopped suet
1 1/3 cups firmly packed brown sugar
½ teaspoon salt
½ teaspoon ground cinnamon

¼ teaspoon ground cloves
¼ teaspoon ground ginger
¼ teaspoon ground nutmeg
2 eggs, well beaten
2/3 cup orange juice
2/3 cup water
1 1/3 cups chopped raisins
1 1/3 cups chopped mixed candid fruit
1 1/3 cups currants
2/3 cup finely chopped figs
Commercial hard sauce

Directions

In a large bowl, combine first 8 ingredients; mix well. Add eggs, orange juice and water; stir well. Combine raisins, candied fruit, currants and figs; add to flour mixture, stirring well. Spoon mixture into greased; 1 ½-quart steamed pudding mold; cover tightly.
2. Place mold on a shallow rack in a large, deep kettle with enough boiling water to come two-thirds up the mold. Cover kettle; steam pudding about 5 hours in continuously boiling water. (Replace water as needed). Let pudding stand 5 minutes; unmold and serve with hard sauce.
Makes 10 to 12 servings

Flamed Plum Pudding

½ cup butter, softened
1 ½ cups firmly packed brown sugar
2 eggs beaten
1 teaspoon vanilla extract
1 cup scraped, grated carrots

1 cup raisins
1 cup dried figs, chopped
1 cup pecans, chopped
½ cup currants
1 cup all-purpose flour
1 teaspoon baking soda
½ teaspoon salt
1 teaspoon ground cinnamon
1 teaspoon ground ginger
½ teaspoon ground allspice
¼ teaspoon ground nutmeg
1 cup fine, dry breadcrumbs
1/8 cup brandy
1/8 cup sherry
¼ cup plus 2 Tablespoons brandy, divided

Directions

1. Cream butter; gradually add sugar, beating well. Add eggs and vanilla; beat well. Stir in next 5 ingredients, mixing well. Combine flour, soda, salt and spices; add to creamed mixture. Stir in breadcrumbs, 1/8 cup brandy and sherry. Stir until all ingredients are combined.
2. Spoon mixture into a well-greased 1 ½ -quart steamed pudding mold; cover mold tightly.
3. Place mold on a shallow rack in a large deep kettle with enough boiling water to come halfway up mold. Cover kettle; steam pudding 3 hours in continuously boiling water. (Replace water as needed).
4. Let pudding stand 5 minutes; unmold onto serving plate. Pour 2 Tablespoons brandy over hot pudding. Heat remaining ¼ cup brandy in a small saucepan to produce fumes (Do Not Boil): ignite and pour over pudding. Chill overnight.
Makes 10 to 12 Servings

Belgian Mocha Cake

½ cup sugar
3 Tablespoons water
2 (1-oz) squares unsweetened chocolate
¾ cup butter or margarine, softened
2 cups sugar
1 teaspoon vanilla extract
4 eggs, separated
2 ¼ cups cake flour
½ teaspoon baking soda
½ teaspoon salt
1 cup milk
1 teaspoon cream of tartar
Mocha frosting (recipe follows)
Chocolate curls or grated chocolate, optional

Directions

1. In a heavy saucepan, combine sugar, water and chocolate; cook over low heat, stirring until chocolate melts. Remove from heat; cool.
2. Cream butter; gradually add sugar, beating well, stir in vanilla. Add egg yolks, one at a time; beating well after each addition. Stir in chocolate mixture.
3. Combine flour, Soda and salt; add to creamed mixture alternately with milk, beginning and ending with flour mixture. Mix well after each addition. Beat in egg whites (at room temperature) until frothy; add cream of tartar, and beat until stiff peaks form. Fold into batter.

4. Grease Three 9-inch round cake pans; line with greased wax paper, and dust with flour. Pour batter into prepared pans, and bake at 350 degrees F. for 25 to 30 minutes or until toothpick inserted in center comes out clean.
5. Spread mocha frosting between layers and on top and sides of cake. Store in refrigerator, or the cake may be frozen. Garnish: with chocolate curls or grated chocolate, if desires.

Mocha Frosting

1 cup butter, softened
2 to 2 ¼ cups powdered sugar
1 Tablespoon instant coffee granules
¾ teaspoon cocoa
¾ teaspoon hot water
2 egg yolks
1 to 1 ½ Tablespoons almond extract
2 Tablespoons rum

Directions

Cream butter with 1½ cups powdered sugar, until lightly and fluffy. Combine coffee granules, cocoa and hot water; stir into creamed mixture. Add egg yolks and beat for 5 minutes. Stir in almond extract and rum. Add enough of remaining powdered sugar to make spreading consistency (frosting gets firm when refrigerated).
Makes enough for one 9-inch layer cake

Black Walnut Cake

½ cup butter
½ cup shortening
2 cups sugar
5 eggs, separated
1 cup buttermilk
1 teaspoon baking soda
2 cups all-purpose flour
1 teaspoon vanilla extract

1 ½ cups chopped black walnut
½ cup (3-oz) flaked coconut
½ teaspoon cream of tartar
Cream cheese frosting
Chopped black walnuts
Red and green candied cherries, diced

Directions

1. Cream butter and shortening; gradually add sugar, beating until light and fluffy and sugar dissolves. Add egg yolks, beating well.
2. Combine buttermilk and soda; stir until soda dissolves.
3. Add flour to creamed mixture alternately with buttermilk mixture, beginning and ending with flour. Stir in vanilla. Add 1 ½ cups walnuts and coconut, stirring well.
4. Beat eggs whites (at room temperature) with cream of tartar until stiff peaks form. Fold egg whites into batter.
5. Pour batter into 3 greased and floured 9-inch round cake pans. Bake at 350 degree F. for 30 minutes or until toothpick inserted in center comes out clean. Cool in pans 10 minutes; remove layers from pans and let cool completely on wire racks.
6. Spread cream cheese frosting between layers and on top and sides of cake; decorate with additional walnuts and candied cherries.
Makes one 3 layer cake

Cream Cheese Frosting

¾ cup butter
1 (8-oz) pkg. cream cheese, softened
1 (3-oz) pkg. cream cheese, softened
6 ¼ cups sifted powdered sugar
1 ½ teaspoons vanilla

Directions

Cream butter and cream cheese; gradually add powdered sugar, beating until light and fluffy. Stir in vanilla.
Makes enough for one 9-inch layer cake

Fig Preserve Cake

1 ½ cups sugar
2 cups all-purpose flour
1 teaspoon baking soda
1 teaspoon salt
1 teaspoon nutmeg
1 teaspoon ground cinnamon
½ teaspoon ground allspice
½ teaspoon ground cloves
1 cup vegetable oil
3 eggs
1 cup buttermilk
1 Tablespoon vanilla extract
1 cup fig preserves, chopped
½ cup chopped pecans or walnuts
Buttermilk Glaze

Directions

In a large mixing bowl, combine dry ingredients; add oil, beating well. Add eggs, and beat well; add buttermilk and vanilla, mixing thoroughly. Stir in preserves and pecans.

Pour batter into a greased and floured 10-inch tube pan; bake at 350 degrees F. for 1 hour and 15 minutes. Cool in pan 10 minutes; remove from pan. Pour warm Buttermilk Glaze over warm cake.
Makes one 10-inch cake

Buttermilk Glaze

¼ cup buttermilk
½ cup sugar
¼ teaspoon baking soda
1 ½ teaspoons cornstarch
¼ cup margarine
1 ½ teaspoons vanilla extract

Directions

Combine first 5 ingredients in a saucepan; bring to a boil, and remove from heat. Cool slightly, stir in vanilla.
Makes enough frosting for one 10-inch cake

Italian Cream Cake

This delicious cake will make raves with your family and friends.

½ cup butter or margarine
½ cup shortening
2 cups sugar
5 large eggs, separated
1 Tablespoon vanilla extract
2 cups all-purpose flour
1 teaspoon baking soda
1 cup buttermilk
1 cup flaked coconut
Nutty cream frosting
Garnishes: Toasted pecan halves, chopped nuts

Directions

1. Beat butter and shortening at medium speed with an electric mixer until fluffy; gradually add sugar, beating well. Add egg

yolks, one at a time, beating until blended after each addition. Add vanilla; beat until blended.

2. Combine flour and soda; add to butter mixture alternately with buttermilk. Beginning and ending with flour mixture. Beat on low speed until blended after each addition. Stir in coconut.

3. Beat egg whites until soft peaks form, fold into batter. Pour batter into 3 greased and floured 9-inch round cake pans.

4. Bake at 350 degrees F. for 25 minutes or until tooth pick inserted in center comes out clean. Cool in pans on wire racks 10 minutes, remove from pans, and cool on wire racks.

5. Spread nutty Cream Cheese Frosting between layers and on top and sides of cake. Garnish, if desired.

Makes one 3 layer cake

Nutty Cream Cheese Frosting

1 cup chopped pecans
1 (8-oz) pkg. cream cheese, softened
½ cup butter or margarine, softened
1 Tablespoon vanilla extract
1 (16-oz) p.kg. Powdered sugar, sifted

Directions

Place pecans in shallow pan; bake at 350 degrees F. for 5 to 10 minutes or until toasted, (be careful not to burn them) stirring occasionally. Cool

Beat cream cheese, butter and vanilla at medium speed until creamy. Add powdered sugar; beating at low speed until blended. Beat at high speed until smooth; stir in pecans. Makes about 4 cups

Pumpkin-Pecan Tube Cake

1 cup granulated sugar
1 cup packed brown sugar
¾ cup shortening
2 eggs
2 ½ cups all-purpose flour
2 teaspoons baking soda
2 teaspoons ground cinnamon
1 teaspoon ground cloves
1 teaspoon ground nutmeg
¼ teaspoon salt
1 (15-oz) can pumpkin solids
1 cup raisins
1 cup chopped pecans or other nuts

1 cup chopped maraschino cherries
Orange juice (optional)
Coarse sugar (optional)
Maraschino cherries (optional)

Directions

1. In a large mixing bowl beat sugar, brown sugar, shortening, and eggs with an electric mixer on medium speed for 2 minutes, scraping bowl occasionally. In medium bowl; mix flour, baking soda, cinnamon, cloves, nutmeg, and salt. Add flour mixture and pumpkin alternately to shortening mixture, beating on low speed after each addition until combined. Stir in raisins, nuts, and cherries.
2. Turn batter into a greased and floured 10-inch fluted tube pan. Bake in a 350 degree F oven about 1 hour or until a toothpick inserted near center comes out clean. Cool on a wire rack for 10 minutes. Remove from pan. Cool completely on wire rack. Brush with orange juice and sprinkle with sugar, if desired. Garnish with maraschino cherries, if desired. Makes 14 to 16 servings

Make-Ahead Recipe
Refrigerate cake, covered, up to 3 days. Or freeze, wrapped in foil, up to 2 months.
Makes 14 Servings

Brandied Fruit Cake

1/8 cup chopped dried cherries
1/8 cup chopped dried mango
1/4 cup dried cranberries
1/4 cup dried currants

2 tablespoons chopped candied citron
1/4 cup brandy
1/2 cup butter
1/4 cup packed brown sugar
1 egg
1/2 cup all-purpose flour
1/8 teaspoon baking soda
1/4 teaspoon salt
1/4 teaspoon ground cinnamon
1/4 cup molasses
2 tablespoons milk
1/4 cup chopped pecans
1/4 cup brandy, divided

Directions

1. Soak cherries, mango, cranberries, currants, and citron in ¼ cup brandy for at least 24 hours. Cover tightly, and store at room temperature.
2. Preheat oven to 325 degrees F. Butter a 6x3-inch round pan or 8x4-inch loaf pan and line it with parchment paper.
3. In a large bowl, cream together butter and brown sugar until light and fluffy. Beat in egg. Whisk together flour, baking soda, salt, and cinnamon; mix into butter and sugar in three batches, alternating with molasses and milk. Stir in soaked fruit and chopped nuts. Spoon batter into prepared pan
4. Bake in preheated oven for 40 to 45 minutes. Cool in the pan for 10 minutes, then sprinkle with 2 tablespoons brandy.
5. Cut out one piece parchment paper and one piece cheesecloth, each large enough to wrap around the cake. Moisten cheesecloth with 1 tablespoon brandy. Arrange cheesecloth on top of parchment paper, and unmold cake onto it. Sprinkle top and sides of cake with remaining brandy. Wrap the cheesecloth closely to the surface of the cake, then wrap with paper. Place in an airtight tin, and age for at least 10 weeks.

If storing longer, douse with additional brandy for every 10 weeks of storage.

Chapter 9: Dips, Sauces and Spreads

Hot Crab Dip

1 (8-oz) cream cheese
1 cup mayonnaise or salad dressing
2 Tablespoons lemon juice
1 teaspoon Worcestershire sauce
¼ to ½ teaspoon Old Bay seasoning
1 Pound lump crabmeat
Garnishes:
Sweet red pepper strips
Parsley sprigs

Directions

Melt cream cheese in a heavy saucepan over low heat, stirring constantly, until cheese melts. Stir in mayonnaise, lemon juice, Worcestershire sauce and old bay seasoning. Add crabmeat and cook over low heat until thoroughly heated. Transfer to a chafing dish, and keep warm. Serve with crackers and garnish; if desired.
Makes 2 ½ cups

Curry Onion Dip

2 cups mayonnaise or salad dressing
3 Tablespoons grated onion
2 Tablespoons tarragon vinegar

2 Tablespoon Chile sauce
1 Tablespoon freeze-dried chives
2 teaspoons curry powder
½ teaspoon salt
¼ teaspoon dried thyme
1/8 teaspoon black pepper
Garnish:
Chopped green onion tops. If desired

Directions

Combine first 9 ingredients; cover and refrigerate 8 hour or overnight. Serve with vegetables or boiled shrimp. Garnish with green onions, if desired.
Makes 2 ¼ cups

Blue Cheese Dip

1 1/3 cups crumbled blue cheese, divided
1 cup margarine (2 sticks)
¼ cup ketchup
2 Tablespoons sugar
2 Tablespoons vegetable oil
2 Tablespoons white vinegar
1 teaspoon dry mustard
½ teaspoon salt
½ teaspoon paprika
¼ teaspoon celery seeds (optional)

Directions

In the container of electric mixer, combine ¾ cup blue cheese and remaining ingredients; process until smooth, stopping once to scrape down sides. Pour mixture in to a bowl, stir in hale the remaining blue cheese. Cover and refrigerate 8 hours. Serve in a hollow cabbage head, if desired. Sprinkle with remaining blue cheese.
Makes 2 cups

Antipasto Dip

1 (14-oz) can artichoke hearts, drained and chopped
2 (4-oz) cans sliced mushrooms, drained and chopped
1 (4oz) jar diced pimientos, drained
1 cup pimiento-stuffed olives, chopped
½ cup chopped green pepper
½ cup chopped celery
½ cup vegetable oil
½ cup finely chopped onion
1 garlic clove, minced
2/3 cup white vinegar
2 ½ teaspoons Italian seasoning
2 teaspoon sugar
½ teaspoon freshly ground pepper

Directions

Combine artichoke hearts and next 5 ingredients in a bowl; set aside. Heat oil in a saucepan over medium heat; add onions and garlic, and cook for 3 minutes or until tender. Add vinegar and

remaining ingredients; bring to a boil. Pour over vegetables; cover and refrigerate 8 hours or overnight. Serve on fresh endive leaves or crackers, if desired.
Makes 5 Cups

Nacho Dip

1 (8-oz) pkg. cream cheese
1 (15-oz) can chili without beans
1 (4-oz) can chopped green Chiles, drained
1 ½ cups (6-oz) shredded sharp cheddar cheese

Directions

Place cream cheese in a 9-inch pie plate. Microwave on medium-low (30%power) 2 ½ to 2 minutes or until softened; spread evenly over bottom of pie plate. Spread chili evenly over cream cheese; cover tightly with plastic wrap, folding back a small edge at allow steam to escape.

Microwave: at High 1 to 2 minutes. Sprinkle with Chiles and cheddar cheese; cover and microwave at High 1 to 2 minutes. Serve dip with tortilla chips
Makes 3 ½ cups

Sweet and Spicy Mustard Dip

2 Tablespoons Mayonnaise
3 Tablespoon course-grained mustard
2 teaspoons sugar

Directions

Combine all ingredients in a 1 cup liquid measuring cup; Microwave on High for 30 seconds, stirring once. Serve with chicken nuggets or strips.
Makes 1/3 cup

Quick Jalapeño Pepper Jelly

Serve as an easy appetizer with cream cheese and crackers.

4 (16-oz) jars lime marmalade or apple jelly
6 to 8 jalapeños peppers, minced
¼ cup apple cider vinegar

Directions

Combine all ingredients in a large saucepan; bring mixture to a boil. Reduce heat and simmer 5 minutes. Remove from heat, Cool. Cover and store in refrigerator up to 2 weeks.
Makes 4 ½ cups

Southwestern Salsa with Black Beans and Corn

Serve with tortilla chips, fajitas, fish or steak.

2 teaspoons cumin seeds
4 (15-oz) cans black beans, rinsed and drained
2 (15 ¼ -oz.) cans whole kernel corn, drained
2 red bell peppers, seeded and minced
1 purple onion, minced
1 cup minced fresh cilantro
1 cup minced fresh parsley
2/3 cup lime juice
½ cup olive oil
6 garlic cloves, pressed
2 teaspoons dried crushed red pepper
1 teaspoon ground black pepper

Directions

In a small cast-iron skillet over medium heat, cook cumin seeds for 2 to 3 minutes or until browned, stirring often.
In a large bowl, combine cumin seeds, black beans and remaining ingredients, toss well. Cover and store in refrigerator up 2 weeks

Cranberry Chutney

Serve with turkey or as an appetizer with gingersnaps and cream cheese

8 (16-oz) cans jellied whole cranberry sauce

2 cups firmly packed light brown sugar
2 cups chopped dates
2 cups currants or raisins
2 cups slivered almonds
2 cups apple cider vinegar
¼ cup minced crystallized ginger
2 teaspoons allspice

Directions

Combine all ingredients in a large Dutch oven. Bring to a boil, stirring constantly; reduce heat, and simmer 30 minutes, stirring occasionally.
Cool, place in jars, and store in refrigerator up to 2 weeks. For longer storage, pack chutney into hot sterilized jars, filling to ½-inch from top; remove any air bubbles, and wipe jar rims. Cover at once with metal lids, and screw on bands. Process boiling in water bath for 5 minutes
Makes 10 pints

Raspberry Vinaigrette

Serve with fresh spinach salad or as a marinade for chicken.

1 1/3 cups raspberry vinegar
1 1/3 cups seedless raspberry jam
1 1/2 Tablespoons ground coriander
2 teaspoons salt
1 teaspoon pepper
3 cups olive oil (evol is best)

Directions

In blender container, combine first 5 ingredients; process until smooth. Turn blender on **High**; gradually add oil in a slow, steady stream. Cover and store in refrigerator up to 2 weeks.
Makes 4 ½ cups

Cranberry Maple Butter

½ cup water
1 (12-oz) bag fresh or frozen cranberries
½ cup maple syrup
¼ cup plus 2 Tablespoons brown sugar
½ teaspoon ground cinnamon
½ teaspoon vanilla extract

Directions

1. Combine water and cranberries in a large sauce pan. Bring to boil; cover, reduce heat and simmer 5 minutes or until cranberries pop. Place cranberries mixture in a blender or food processor; cover and process until smooth.
2. Combine cranberry mixture, maple syrup, sugar and cinnamon in saucepan; bring to a boil. Reduce heat; simmer, uncovered, 25 minutes or until mixture is thick, stirring frequently. Stir in vanilla. Cool. Store in airtight container in the refrigerator up to 2 weeks
Makes 1 ¾ cups

Dutch-Apple Butter

6 ½ cups peeled, chopped Granny Smith apples (about 2 lbs)
1 ¼ cups apple cider
¾ cup packed brown sugar
¾ teaspoon ground cinnamon
¼ teaspoon ground all spice
¼ teaspoon ground cloves
¼ teaspoon ground ginger

Directions

1. Combine apples and cider in a large saucepan or Dutch oven. Bring to a boil; cover, reduce heat, simmer 40 minutes or until tender. Place apples mixture in a blender or food processor, cover and process until smooth.
2. Combine pureed apple mixture, sugar and remaining ingredients in a saucepan; bring to a boil. Reduce heat, simmer, uncovered, 25 minutes or until mixture is thick, stirring frequently. Cool. Store in an airtight container; in refrigerator up to 2 months.
Makes 3 cups

Breakfast Prune Butter

1 ¾ cups boiling water

2 regular-size tea bags
8 ounces pitted prunes
1/3 cup sugar
1 teaspoon grated lemon rind
½ teaspoon vanilla extract

Directions

1. Combine boiling water and tea bags in a medium a bowl; cover and steep 5 minutes. Discard tea bags.
2. Combine tea and prunes in a large heavy saucepan. Bring to a boil; cover, reduce heat, simmer 5 minutes or until tender. Place prune mixture in a blender; cover and process until smooth.
3. Combine prunes mixture, sugar and lemon rind in a saucepan; bring to a boil. Reduce heat; simmer, uncovered, 20 minutes or until mixture is thick, stirring frequently. Stir in vanilla; cool. Store in airtight container; in refrigerator up to 2 months.
Makes 1 ¾ cups

Spiced Plum Butter

¾ cup orange juice
4 pounds plums, pitted and quartered
1 cup sugar
½ teaspoon ground cinnamon
¼ teaspoon ground allspice
¼ teaspoon ground ginger
1/8 teaspoon ground nutmeg
1/8 teaspoon ground cloves

Directions

1. In a large saucepan, combine orange juice and plums. Bring to a boil; cover, reduce heat, and simmer 30 minutes or until tender. Place mixture in a blender; cover and process until smooth. Press mixture through a fine sieve over a bowl; discard solids.
2. In a saucepan, combine plum mixture, sugar and remaining ingredients; bring to a boil. Reduce heat; simmer, uncovered, 1 hour or until thick, stirring frequently. Cool. Store in an airtight container; in the refrigerator up to 2 months.
Makes 2 ½ cups

Homemade Apple Sauce

10 cups coarsely chopped red cooking apples (about 3 lbs)
1 cup apple cider
½ cup firmly packed brown sugar

Directions

1. Combine all ingredients in a large saucepan. Bring to a boil. Reduce heat; simmer 1 hour or until apples are tender. Stirring occasionally
Makes 10 Servings

Top with a fruit sauce: In just 5 to 15 minutes whip up one of these delicious fruit sauces and turn any meal into a festive treat.

Banana Sundae Sauce

½ cup butter or margarine, melted
1 ½ cups sifted powdered sugar
¼ teaspoon ground cinnamon
1 Tablespoon water
1 teaspoon lemon juice
1 teaspoon vanilla extract
2 cups sliced bananas

Directions

Combine all ingredients except bananas in a medium saucepan, cook over medium heat for 5 minutes or until smooth, stirring occasionally. Stir in bananas. Serve warm over vanilla ice cream or pound cake.
Makes 2 cups

Fresh Cranberry Sauce

4 cups fresh cranberries

2 cups sugar
2 cups water
2 Tablespoons grated orange rind

Directions

Wash cranberries and drain. Combine cranberries, sugar, and water in a medium saucepan; bring to a boil, and cook for 7 to 10 minutes or until cranberry skins pop. Stir in orange peel. Cool. Serve with Poultry or pork.
Makes 4 cups

Raisin Sauce

½ cup finely packed brown sugar
1 ½ Tablespoon all-purpose flour
1 ½ teaspoon dry mustard
1 ½ cups water
2 Tablespoons white vinegar
½ cup raisins

Directions

Combine brown sugar, flour and dry mustard in a medium saucepan, stirring well. Add water vinegar and raisins; cook over low heat, stirring constantly, until thickened. Serve warm over pork
Makes about 2 1/3 cups

Honey-Lemon Mustard Sauce

½ cup butter or margarine
2 Tablespoons honey
1 teaspoon grated lemon rind
1 Tablespoon plus 1 teaspoon lemon juice
1 teaspoon prepared mustard

Directions

In a small saucepan, combine all ingredients. Cook over low heat until thoroughly heated. Serve with vegetables.
Makes about ½ cup

Pineapple Rum Sauce

1 cup firmly packed brown sugar
2 Tablespoons cornstarch
1 1/3 cups pineapple juice
2 Tablespoons butter or margarine
1 ¼ teaspoons rum flavoring

Directions

In a medium saucepan, combine sugar and cornstarch; mix well. Stir in pineapple juice; cook over medium heat, stirring

constantly, until thickened. Remove from heat; stir in butter and rum flavoring. Serve warm or chilled over ice cream or pound cake.
Makes 1 2/3 cups

Chapter 10: Punches and Drinks

Autumn Harvest Punch

2 cups water
1 ½ to 2 cups sugar
4 (3-inch) cinnamon Sticks
36 whole cloves
2 quarts cranberry juice cocktail
1 quart orange juice
1 ½ to 2 cups lemon juice
1 lemon, sliced
1 orange, diced
1 cup rum or 2 Tablespoons rum flavoring

Directions

Combine first 4 ingredients in a large Dutch oven; bring to a boil over high heat. Reduce heat and simmer 7 minutes; remove and discard spices.
Add cranberry juice and remaining ingredients; cook over medium heat until thoroughly heated.
Makes 5 quarts

Berry-Colada Punch

1 (16oz) pkg. frozen strawberries, thawed
1 (15-oz) can cream of coconut
3 cups pineapple juice, chilled
3 cups club soda, chilled
2 cups rum, optional

Directions

Combine strawberries and cream of coconut in container of electric blender, and process until smooth; pour into a pitcher or large bowl. Stir in pineapple juice, club soda and rum, if desired. Serve over crushed ice.
Makes 2 ½ quarts

Golden Fruit Punch

2/3 cup boiling water
3 regular-size tea bags
1 ½ cups pineapple juice
1 cup grapefruit juice1 cup orange juice
½ cup lemon juice
1 ¼ cups sugar
4 cups ginger ale, chilled

2 cups ice water

Directions

Pour boiling water over tea bags; cover at let stand for 5 minutes. Remove and discard tea bags.

Combine tea and fruit juices in a large pitcher or bowl; add sugar, stir until dissolved. Cover and chill.

Stir in ginger ale and ice water; serve immediately
Makes 2 ½ quarts

Fruit Juice Punch

1 (12-oz) can frozen orange juice concentrate, thawed
1 (12-oz) can frozen lemonade concentrate, thawed
1 (12-oz) can frozen limeade concentrate, thawed
4 cup cold water
1 liter ginger ale, chilled
orange, lemon, or lime slices – garnish

Directions

In punch bowl or 2 ½ quart pitcher, combine concentrates and water; mix well. Stir in ginger ale; serve immediately. Garnish with fruit slices, if desired.

Sunset Punch

1 quart cranberry juice cocktail
1 quart pink lemonade
1 quart orange juice
1 quart pineapple juice
1 quart ginger ale, chilled
1 quart raspberry sherbet or sorbet

Directions

Combine first 4 ingredients in a large bowl. Stir in ginger ale; scoop sherbet into punch. Serve immediately
Makes 1 ½ gallons

Cranberry Punch

1 package lemonade drink mix (2-quart size)
5 cup cold water
1 bottle (32 oz) cranberry juice cocktail, chilled
3/4 cup vodka, optional
1 lemon and orange, sliced
Ice cubes

Directions

In large pitcher, add drink mix then water; stir to dissolve. Add

cranberry juice and vodka, if desired. Garnish with lemon and orange slices if desired.
Twelve 1-cup servings

Christmas Punch

2 cups boiling water
¾ cup sugar
½ teaspoon ground cinnamon
1 (46-oz) can pineapple juice, chilled
1 (32-oz) bottle cranberry juice, chilled
1 (28-oz) bottle ginger ale, chilled

Directions

1. Combine water, sugar and cinnamon in a saucepan, bring to a boil, stir until sugar dissolves, and chill.
2. Combine sugar syrup mixture, pineapple juice, cranberry juice and ginger ale. Serve over ice
Makes about 3 ¾ -quarts

Mocha Coffee

4 oz. chocolate
2 Tablespoons Kahlua

1 cup strong coffee (hot)
Whipped cream

Directions

Melt chocolate. Gradually add Kahlua and coffee
Pour in to cups, top with whipped cream
Makes 2 Servings

White Russian Coffee

One brewed pot of French Vanilla or Crème Brulee coffee,
1 cup heavy cream,
1½ cups coffee flavored liqueur,
Garnish: chocolate shavings, ground chocolate, or cocoa mixed with powdered sugar.

Directions

Brew coffee, and then stir in heavy cream and liqueur. Top with garnish of ground chocolate or cocoa, or chocolate shavings, if desired
Makes 12 Servings (5-oz)

Irish Coffee Nog

3 Tablespoons instant coffee granules
1 cup Irish whiskey or bourbon
2 quarts eggnog
1/3 cup firmly packed brown sugar
½ teaspoon ground cinnamon
½ teaspoon ground nutmeg
1 quart coffee ice cream

Directions

In a large bowl, dissolve coffee in whiskey; add eggnog, brown sugar, cinnamon and nutmeg. Beat at low speed with an electric mixer until smooth. Cover: chill 1 hour. Pour into a punch bowl, top with scoops of ice cream.
Makes 3 ½ quarts

Note: For individual servings, pour eggnog mixture into mugs, and top with a scoop of ice cream.

Mexican Mocha

3 cups milk
1 (12-oz) can evaporated milk
1/3 cup chocolate syrup
1 Tablespoon instant coffee granules
6 (3-inch sticks) cinnamon sticks
1 ¼ cups frozen whipped topping, thawed

Directions

Combine milk, evaporated milk, chocolate syrup and coffee granules in a 2 quart container. Cover tightly with plastic wrap; fold back a small edge to allow steam to escape. Microwave on Medium (50% power) 4 to 8 minutes or until steaming, stirring once. To serve, pour into 6 individual mugs; add a cinnamon stick, Top each mug with 1/3 cup whipped topping.
Makes 6 cups

Mexican Rice Drink (Horchata)

¾ cup of rice, ground finely to a powder
¾ cup almonds, peeled
½ teaspoon cinnamon
1 teaspoon lime zest
4 cups very hot water
1 ½ cup sugar
1 teaspoon vanilla

Directions:

1.   Place the rice, almonds, cinnamon, lime and hot water in a pot. Cover and leave overnight. The next day, place all the ingredients in blender.

2.   Add in the sugar and vanilla and blend well. Strain the rice drink. Serve Mexican drink over ice and sprinkle a little cinnamon.

Milk Punch

This punch is lighter in calories and texture, and it's simple to make. I serve it during the holiday season, either in the late afternoon or after dinner. It's like a delicious adult milkshake.

1½ cups dark rum
¾ cup brandy
3 Tablespoons vanilla extract
1 ½ cups sugar
3 quarts whole milk
Ground nutmeg for garnish

Directions

Combine rum, brandy and vanilla in a large pitcher and stir in sugar until dissolved. Stir in milk. Freeze until very cold or even slushy. For at least 4 hours.

To serve, pour into glasses and sprinkle with nutmeg.
Makes 12 drinks

Bug Juice

Here's a look-alike nonalcoholic version of the Cosmopolitan

1 (12-oz) can frozen limeade concentrate

½ cup cranberry juice
1 (65-oz) bottle ginger ale, chilled
Marshmallows for garnish, optional

Directions

Add limeade concentrate and cranberry juice to pitcher of ice and stir to blend. Stir in ginger ale, and serve, adding a few marshmallow, if desired, to each glass
Makes 8 drinks

Chapter 11: Leftover Ham and Turkey Recipes

Cheesy Ham and Potato Casserole

2 Tablespoons chopped onion
¼ cup butter or margarine
¼ cup all-purpose flour
1 teaspoon salt
½ teaspoon dry mustard
Dash pepper
1½ cups milk
2 cups (8-oz) cheddar cheese, shredded, divided
2 cups cooked ham 6 cups cooked potatoes

Directions

In a large saucepan; melt butter, sauté onion until tender. Add flour, salt, dry mustard and pepper, stirring until smooth. Cook 1 minute, stirring constantly. Gradually add milk; cook over medium heat, stirring constantly, until thickened and bubbly. Add 1 ½ cups cheese, stirring until cheese melts. Add ham and potatoes, tossing gently. Spoon: mixture into a greased 2-quart shallow baking dish, bake, uncovered; at 350 degrees F. for 25 minutes. Sprinkle with remaining ½ cup cheese; bake an additional 5 minutes.
Makes 6 servings

Ham and Vegetable Quiche

Pastry for 10-inch pie
½ cup chopped cauliflower
¼ cup chopped carrots
¼ cup chopped onion
¼ cup chopped green pepper
1/3 cup chopped ham
1 cup (4-oz) shredded cheddar cheese
3 eggs beaten
1 cup milk
½ teaspoon salt
Fresh parsley sprigs

Directions

1. Line a 10-inch dish with pastry; Trim excess pastry around edges. Prick bottom and sides with a fork; bake at 425 degrees F. for 5 minutes; cool.
2. Cook next 4 ingredients in boiling salted water to cover 5 minutes or until tender-crisp; drain well. Layer ham and vegetables in pastry shell; sprinkle with cheese. Combine eggs, milk and salt; beat well. Pour into pastry shell; Bake at 375 degrees F. for 40 to 45 minutes or until set. Let stand 10 minutes before serving. Garnish with parsley sprigs
Makes one 10-inch quiche

Ham Salad with Tortillas

1 cup diced ham
1 large head romaine lettuce, chopped
1/3 cup diced red onion
1/2 cup chopped pecans or roasted peanuts
1/2 cup cooked chick peas
1 medium cucumber peeled and diced
2 small to medium tomatoes, diced
1 cup diced Havarti, Monterey Jack, or mild Cheddar cheese
1 Tablespoon chopped fresh parsley

Vinaigrette
¼ cup balsamic vinegar
1 teaspoon honey Dijon mustard
½ cup olive oil
Salt and pepper:
Tortilla chips

Directions

Heat a skillet, spray with vegetable cooking spray or a little butter then brown ham. Combine ham with the chopped lettuce, onion, pecans, chickpeas, cucumber, tomato, cheese, and parsley; toss to mix well.
In a measuring cup or small bowl, combine the balsamic vinegar and mustard. Gradually whisk in the olive oil; season with salt and pepper to taste. Arrange on individual salad plates on a bed of tortilla chips with dressing on the side.

Turkey and Dressing Pie

2 ½ cups cornbread dressing
3 Tablespoons butter or margarine
1 ½ cups finely chopped cooked turkey
1 cup (4-oz) shredded Swiss cheese
4 eggs
1/3 cup half and half or milk

Directions

1. Combine dressing and butter; mix well. Press on bottom and sides of a 9-inch quiche dish. Bake at 400 degrees F. for 5 to 7 minutes. Cool.
2. Combine turkey and cheese; spread on cornbread shell. Combine eggs and half and half; beat well. Pour over turkey mixture; Bake at 325 degrees F. for 35 to 40 minutes or until pie is set.

Makes one 9-inch pie

Turkey al La King

¼ cup butter
½ cup chopped green pepper
4 ounces sliced mushrooms
¼ cup flour
1 ½ cups half-and-half or milk
1 can (10¾ -oz) condensed cream of mushroom soup
1 (2 ounces) jar pimiento strips or chopped
2 ½ cups cooked cubed turkey
1/8 teaspoon onion powder
1/8 teaspoon pepper

Directions

In skillet; melt butter; add green pepper and mushrooms. Cover and simmer 5 minutes. Remove vegetables with slotted spoon. Add flour to butter, cooking and stirring until smooth. Add half-and-half and cream of mushroom soup, stirring until smooth and thickened. Add turkey, pimiento, mushrooms, green pepper, and seasonings, and adjust seasonings to taste. Serve over hot cooked rice, noodles, biscuits, or toast
Makes 6 Servings

Conclusion

Thank you for purchasing Thanksgiving and Christmas recipes; it's been fun sharing these recipes with you. I trust you have found some new holiday favorites.

Part 2

Introduction

Welcome and thank you for downloading my book!

You will surely adore each recipe here from its first to last as they will for sure astonish you with new flavours and all have clickable links in the table of contents so it's easy to find them.

Slow Cooker Corn Chowder

Ingredients
1 tablespoon vegetable oil
1 cup finely chopped carrots (2 medium)
1/2 cup finely chopped celery (1 stalk)
1/3 cup finely chopped onion (1 small)
3 cups peeled and cubed russet potatoes (about 1 pound)
3 cups reduced-sodium chicken broth
1 bay leaf
3/4 teaspoon salt
3/4 teaspoon dried thyme, crushed
1/8 teaspoon paprika
4 cups frozen whole kernel corn
2 cups milk
3 tablespoons cornstarch
2 tablespoons dry white wine
1 tablespoon snipped fresh thyme
4 slices bacon, crisp-cooked, drained, and crumbled
Cracked black pepper

Instructions
In a medium saucepan heat oil over medium-high heat. Add carrots, celery, and onion; cook about 7 minutes or until vegetables are tender, stirring occasionally. Transfer mixture to a 4- to 6-quart slow cooker. Stir in potatoes, broth, bay leaf, salt, dried thyme, and paprika.

Cover and cook on low-heat setting about 3 hours or on high-heat setting about 1-1/2 hours or until potatoes are tender. Stir in corn and milk. Cover and cook about 1 hour or until heated through.

In a small bowl stir together cornstarch and wine; stir into mixture in cooker. Cover and cook for 10 minutes more. Stir in fresh thyme.

Using a potato masher, gently mash potatoes until soup is slightly thickened. Sprinkle each serving with crumbled bacon and cracked pepper.

2. Moist & Tender Turkey Breast

Ingredients
1 bone-in turkey breast (6 to 7 pounds)
4 fresh rosemary sprigs
4 garlic cloves, peeled
1/2 cup water
1 tablespoon brown sugar
1/2 teaspoon coarsely ground pepper
1/4 teaspoon salt

Instructions
Place turkey breast, rosemary, garlic and water in a 6-qt. slow cooker. Mix brown sugar, pepper and salt; sprinkle over turkey.

Cook, covered, on low 4-6 hours or until turkey is tender and a thermometer inserted in turkey reads at least 170°. Yield: 12 servings.

3. Gingerbread Pudding Cake

Ingredients
1/2 cup molasses
1 cup water
1/4 cup butter, softened
1/4 cup sugar
1 large egg white
1 teaspoon vanilla extract
1-1/4 cups all-purpose flour
3/4 teaspoon baking soda

1/4 teaspoon salt
1/2 teaspoon ground cinnamon
1/2 teaspoon ground ginger
1/4 teaspoon ground allspice
1/8 teaspoon ground nutmeg
1/2 cup chopped pecans
6 tablespoons brown sugar
3/4 cup hot water
2/3 cup butter, melted
Sweetened whipped cream, optional

Instructions

Mix molasses and 1 cup water. In a bowl, cream softened butter and sugar until light and fluffy; beat in egg white and vanilla. In another bowl, whisk together flour, baking soda, salt and spices; add to creamed mixture alternately with molasses mixture, beating well after each addition. Fold in pecans.

Pour into a greased 3-qt. slow cooker. Sprinkle with brown sugar. Mix hot water and melted butter; pour over batter (do not stir).

Cook, covered, on high until a toothpick inserted in center comes out clean, 2 to 2-1/2 hours.
Turn off slow cooker; let stand 15 minutes. If desired, serve with whipped cream. Yield: 8 servings.

4. Green Bean Casserole

Ingredients
2 packages (16 ounces each) frozen cut green beans, thawed
2 cans (10-3/4 ounces each) condensed cream of mushroom soup, undiluted
1 can (8 ounces) sliced water chestnuts, drained
1 cup 2% milk
6 bacon strips, cooked and crumbled
1 teaspoon pepper
1/8 teaspoon paprika
4 ounces process cheese (Velveeta), cubed
1 can (2.8 ounces) French-fried onions

Instructions
In a 4-qt. slow cooker, combine the green beans, soup, water chestnuts, milk, bacon, pepper and paprika.

Cover and cook on low for 5-6 hours or until beans are tender; stir in cheese. Cover and cook for 30 minutes or until cheese is melted. Sprinkle with onions. Yield: 10 servings.

5. Hot Mulled Ginger-Spiced Cider

Ingredients
3 whole cloves
2 (1 x 4-inch) strips orange rind
2 whole allspice
1 (3-inch) cinnamon stick
1 (1/2-inch) piece peeled fresh ginger
12 cups apple cider
1/2 cup apple jelly
1/4 teaspoon ground nutmeg

Instructions

Place the first 5 ingredients on a 5-inch-square double layer of cheesecloth. Gather edges of cheesecloth together; tie securely.

Place cheesecloth bag, cider, jelly, and nutmeg in an electric slow cooker. Cover and cook on high for 4 hours. Remove and discard cheesecloth bag.

6. Grandma Dean's Chicken and Dressing

Ingredients
1 (2 1/2-pound) rotisserie chicken, skinned, boned, and shredded (about 4 cups)
6 cups coarsely crumbled cornbread
8 (1-ounce) firm white bread slices, torn into pieces
2 (14-ounce) cans chicken broth
2 (10 3/4-ounce) cans cream of chicken soup
1 medium onion, chopped
3 celery ribs, chopped
4 large eggs, lightly beaten
2 teaspoons ground sage
1/2 teaspoon pepper
1/4 teaspoon salt
1/2 cup butter, softened

Instructions
Combine first 11 ingredients in a large bowl.

Transfer mixture to a lightly greased 5-quart round slow cooker. Dot evenly with butter.

Cover and cook on HIGH 3 to 4 hours or on LOW 7 hours or until set. Stir well before serving.

7. Steamed Brown Bread with Currants and Walnuts

Ingredients
1/2 cup all-purpose flour
1/2 cup whole-wheat flour
1/2 cup yellow cornmeal
3/4 teaspoon ground cinnamon
1/2 teaspoon baking soda

1/2 teaspoon salt
1 cup low-fat buttermilk
1/3 cup molasses
1/2 cup dried currants
2 tablespoons chopped walnuts
Vegetable cooking spray

Instructions

Combine the first 6 ingredients in a large bowl, and make a well in center of mixture. Combine buttermilk and molasses; stir well. Add to flour mixture, stirring just until moistened. Fold in currants and walnuts.

Spoon the mixture into a 13-ounce coffee can coated with cooking spray. Cover with aluminum foil coated with cooking spray; secure foil with a rubber band. Place the can in an electric slow cooker; add enough hot water to cooker to come halfway up sides of can.

Cover with lid, and cook on high-heat setting for 2 hours and 50 minutes or until a wooden pick inserted in center comes out clean. Remove can from water. Let bread cool, covered, in can on a wire rack for 5 minutes. Remove bread from can, and let cool completely on wire rack.

8. Butternut Squash Soup

Ingredients
2 cups vegetable stock
2 cloves garlic, peeled and minced
1 carrot, peeled and diced
1 Granny Smith apple, cored and diced
1 medium (uncooked) butternut squash, peeled, seeded and diced
1 sprig fresh sage
1 white onion, diced
1/2 teaspoon salt, or more to taste
1/4 teaspoon freshly-ground black pepper, or more to taste
1/8 teaspoon cayenne, or more to taste
pinch of ground cinnamon and nutmeg
1/2 cup canned coconut milk
(optional garnishes: extra coconut milk and cayenne)

Instructions
Add vegetable stock, garlic, carrot, apple, butternut squash, sage, onion, salt, pepper, cayenne, cinnamon and nutmeg to a slow cooker. Toss to combine.

Cook for 6-8 hours on low, or 3-4 hours on high, or until the squash is completely tender and mashes easily with a fork. Stir in the coconut milk.

Use an immersion blender to puree the soup until smooth. (Or you can transfer the soup in two batches into a traditional blender, and puree until smooth, being very careful when working with the hot liquid.) Taste, and season with additional salt, pepper and cayenne if needed.

Serve warm, with optional garnishes if desired.

9. Mashed Potatoes

Ingredients
3 pounds Yukon Gold or Red potatoes, roughly chopped into 1-inch pieces and peeled if desired
1 cup chicken or vegetable stock
1/4 cup butter, cut into small cubes
3 cloves garlic, minced
1/2 cup plain Greek yogurt or sour cream
1/2 teaspoon salt
1/4 teaspoon black pepper
1/3 - 1/2 cup milk, warmed
(optional add-ins: crumbled bacon bits, shredded cheddar cheese, crumbled blue cheese, chopped green onions or chives, etc.)

Instructions
Add potatoes and stock to the bowl of a slow cooker, and place butter cubes and minced garlic on top.

Cover and cook on high for 3-4 hours, or on low for 7-8 hours, or until the potatoes are cooked and soft.

Use a potato masher or an electric mixer to mash the potatoes to your desired consistency. Stir in the Greek yogurt (or sour cream), salt, and black pepper.

And add your desired amount of warm milk, until the potatoes reach your desired level of creamy-ness. Stir in any other add-ins if desired.

10. Cranberry-Orange Mulled Wine

Ingredients

1 (750 ml) bottle of Merlot or other fruity (but not too sweet!) red wine such as Cabernet Sauvignon or Zinfandel
2 cups orange juice (I either like squeezing my own or buying a 100% pure fresh-squeezed version)
1 cup fresh or frozen whole cranberries, rinsed and picked through
1/3 cup granulated sugar plus more to taste
1 medium orange (I like to use an organic orange for recipes like this because it will be soaking in the beverage, peel and all)
2 tablespoons whole cloves
2 3-inch cinnamon sticks
1/2 cup brandy
Garnishes, if desired: cinnamon sticks, orange slices, and/or fresh cranberries threaded onto a cocktail pick

Instructions

Add wine, orange juice, cranberries, and sugar to a 3-quart or larger Crock Pot. Stir to help sugar begin to dissolve.

Wash orange thoroughly and stud the orange with the cloves - just stick the cloves directly into the peel, pointy end first. I like to poke it all over with a toothpick first to make holes for the cloves.

Add the clove-studded orange and the cinnamon sticks to the wine.

Cook on low for 2 - 3 hours, or until the berries are tender. You can cook it for an hour or two longer if you wish, but take care that it doesn't boil.

Remove the orange and the cinnamon sticks, then VERY CAREFULLY pour the mulled wine through a fine-mesh sieve into a large heat-proof bowl. Using the back of the spoon, press on the cranberries to get all of the juices into the bowl. A berry or two may burst, so watch out!

Return wine to the Crock Pot and stir in the brandy. Taste and add additional sugar until it's just sweet enough. I like it just past the pucker point; you may prefer a sweeter mulled wine.

Ladle into mugs and serve with a cinnamon stick, an orange slice, and/or fresh cranberries pushed onto a cocktail stick, if desired.

Keep your Crock Pot on the "warm" setting to keep the wine nice and hot. If your Crock Pot doesn't have a warm setting, try alternating between "low" and off.

11. Balsamic Brussels Sprouts

Ingredients
1/2 cup balsamic vinegar
2 tablespoons brown sugar, packed
2 pounds brussels sprouts, trimmed and halved
2 tablespoons olive oil
Kosher salt and freshly ground black pepper
2 tablespoons unsalted butter, cut into cubes
1/4 cup freshly grated Parmesan cheese

Instructions
To make the balsamic reduction, add balsamic vinegar and brown sugar to a small saucepan over medium heat. Bring to a slight boil and reduce by half, about 6-8 minutes; set aside and let cool.

Place brussels sprouts into a 3-qt slow cooker. Stir in olive oil and season with salt and pepper, to taste. Top with butter.

Cover and cook on low heat for 3-4 hours or high for 1-2 hours.

Serve immediately, drizzled with balsamic reduction and topped with Parmesan.

12. Cranberry Sauce

Ingredients

12 ounces fresh cranberries
1/2 cup orange juice
1/2 cup water
1/3 cup sugar (use your desired kind of sugar or sweetener, and add more/less to taste)
optional add-ins: a splash or bourbon or red wine, orange zest, a pinch of ground ginger, a pinch of cinnamon and cloves, some chopped walnuts, or a splash of vanilla extract

Instructions

Add all ingredients to the bowl of a slow cooker and stir to combine.

Cook on high for 3-4 hours or on low for 7-8 hours, or until the cranberries have popped open and the sauce is bubbly. Taste and stir in any extra sweetener or add-ins if desired.

Serve warm. (Heads up that the sauce will thicken considerably as it cools.)

13. Pecan Pie

Ingredients
1 refrigerated pie crust
3 eggs
1 cup sugar
2/3 cup dark corn syrup
1/3 cup melted butter
1/8 teaspoon salt
1 teaspoon vanilla extract
1 1/2 cups chopped pecans (or a combination of chopped and whole pecan halves)
Vanilla ice cream for serving

Instructions
Spray the inside of a crock pot with cooking spray.

Place pie crust in crock pot and mold it to fit the shape of the crock pit. (This is easier if you have a round crock pot instead of an oval one, but you can make do with an oval.)

Stir remaining ingredients together, except pecans, until mixed well.

Stir in pecans. I like to leave about half the pecans to arrange on top of the filling to make it look prettier.

Pour filling into pie crust. If you reserved some pecans, gently place them on top of the filling.

Cover crock pot and cook on HIGH for 2 1/2 to 3 hours.

14. Caramel Apple Crumble

Ingredients
1 cup brown sugar
1/2 cup granulated sugar
5 large apples, cut into chunks
1/4 teaspoon salt
1 teaspoon cinnamon

Topping
2/3 cup oats
2/3 cup loosely packed brown sugar
1/4 cup flour
1/2 teaspoon cinnamon
3-4 tablespoons softened butter
1 teaspoon vanilla extract

Instructions
Toss apple chunks with salt and cinnamon.

In the bottom of your slow-cooker [mine is 7 quarts], mix brown and granulated sugars, then spread evenly to cover. Layer apples on top, keeping them in a single layer as much as possible, then adding the rest of top.

Mix the crumble topping together in a bowl, using your fingers to distribute the butter evenly and thoroughly and clump it together. Sprinkle it over top of the apples. Cook apples on low for 4 hours, or high for 2 hours.

Turn off heat, unplug, and let sit, covered, for one hour. During this time the caramel will thicken a bit more. Serve with vanilla ice cream.

15. Chocolate Cake

Ingredients
2 cups flour
2 cups sugar
5 tablespoons natural unsweetened cocoa powder
5 teaspoons baking powder
1 teaspoon kosher salt
1 cup semisweet chocolate chips
5 tablespoons unsalted butter
1 1/3 cups milk
2 large eggs, beaten
1 teaspoon vanilla extract

Instructions
In the slow cooker, whisk together the flour, sugar, cocoa powder, baking powder, salt, and chocolate chips.

Heat the butter until just melted, then add it to the milk. Add the eggs and vanilla extract. Pour it into the slow cooker.

Mix until everything is combined, making sure that there is no more dry mixture left. Spread the batter evenly in the crock.

Plug in the slow cooker and cook on high for two to two and a half hours.

When you remove the lid, be sure not to let the condensation drip onto the cake.

Turn off the heat and let the cake sit for at least 20 minutes before serving.

16. Sage and Sausage Stuffing Recipe

Ingredients

2 1/2 pounds (about 2 loaves) high quality sandwich bread or soft Italian or French bread, cut into 3/4-inch dice, about 5 quarts
8 tablespoons (1 stick) butter, plus more for buttering slow cooker
1 1/2 pounds sage sausage, removed from casing
1 large onion, finely chopped (about 2 cups)
4 large stalks celery, finely chopped (about 2 cups)
2 cloves garlic, minced or grated on microplane
1/4 cup minced fresh sage leaves (or 2 teaspoons dried sage leaves)
24 ounces (3 cups) low-sodium chicken or turkey broth, preferably homemade
3 whole eggs
1/4 cup minced parsley leaves
Kosher salt and freshly ground black pepper

Instructions

Adjust oven racks to lower middle and upper middle position. Preheat oven to 275°F. Spread bread evenly over two rimmed baking sheets. Stagger trays on oven racks and bake until completely dried, about 50 minutes total, rotating trays and stirring bread cubes several times during baking. Remove from oven and allow to cool. Turn off oven.

In large Dutch oven, melt butter over medium high heat until foaming subsides (don't allow butter to brown), about 2 minutes. Add sausage and mash with stiff whisk or potato masher to break up into fine pieces (largest pieces should be no greater than 1/4-inch). Cook, stirring frequently until only a few bits of pink remain, about 8 minutes. Add onions, celery, garlic, and sage and cook, stirring frequently, until vegetables are softened, about 10 minutes. Remove from heat and add half of chicken stock.

Whisk remaining chicken stock, eggs, and 3 tablespoons parsley in medium bowl until homogeneous. Stirring constantly with wooden spoon, slowly pour egg mixture into sausage mixture. Add bread cubes and fold gently until evenly mixed.

Grease the inside of a slow cooker with butter. Transfer stuffing to slow cooker and set to low heat. Cook for 5 hours. Keep warm or serve.

17. Quinoa-Stuffed Peppers

Ingredients
1 (15-ounce) can white beans
4 scallions
4 large red bell peppers
1 cup cooked quinoa (follow our Basic Quinoa Salad recipe through step 3)
1/2 cup crumbled feta cheese
1 teaspoon kosher salt
Freshly ground black pepper
Hot sauce (optional)

Instructions
Drain and rinse the beans. Cut the scallions into thin slices, roughly separating the mostly white slices from the green ones.

Cut a thin slice off the bottom of each pepper so they'll sit upright in the slow cooker insert.
Slice the tops off of each pepper just below the stem and reserve the tops. Remove the seeds and white veins from inside the peppers.

Take the reserved pepper tops and dice the flesh from around the stems. Discard the stems.

In a mixing bowl, combine the diced pepper tops, quinoa, feta, beans, sliced scallion whites, measured salt, and black pepper to taste.

Stuff the quinoa mixture into the 4 peppers and arrange them so they sit upright in the slow cooker. Cook on high for 4 hours.

Peel off the skin of each pepper (this is optional), and sprinkle the stuffed peppers with the green scallion slices. Serve with the optional hot sauce.

18. Garlic Mashed Potatoes

Ingredients
3 pounds red potatoes, chopped
1/4 cup unsalted butter
4 cloves garlic, crushed and peeled
Kosher salt and freshly ground black pepper, to taste
1/2 cup sour cream
1/3 cup freshly grated Parmesan
2 tablespoons milk, or more, as needed
1/2 teaspoon dried thyme
1/2 teaspoon dried oregano
1/2 teaspoon dried basil
1/4 teaspoon freshly grated nutmeg
2 tablespoons chopped fresh chives

Instructions
Lightly coat the inside of a slow cooker with nonstick spray. Place potatoes, butter, garlic and 1/4 cup water into the slow cooker; season with salt and pepper, to taste. Cover and cook on low heat for 7-8 hours or high heat for 3-4 hours, or until tender.

Add sour cream, Parmesan, milk, thyme, oregano, basil and nutmeg. Using an electric mixer fitted with the paddle attachment, blend potatoes until light and fluffy, about 2-3 minutes. If the mixture is too thick, add more milk as needed until desired consistency is reached.

Serve immediately, garnished with chives, if desired.

19. Pumpkin Cobbler

Ingredients
3 eggs
Large can of pumpkin puree (29 oz)
12 oz evaporated milk
1 cup granulated sugar
1/4 cup brown sugar
2 tsp cinnamon
1/2 tsp ginger
1/2 tsp salt
1 tsp vanilla
Butter Pecan Cake Mix
4 tbsp brown sugar
3/4 cup melted butter

Instructions
Beat the eggs slightly.

Add the pumpkin puree, evaporated milk, sugars, cinnamon, ginger, salt and vanilla.

Pour the mixture into a greased slow cooker.

Top with the powdered cake mix and sprinkle with brown sugar.

Drizzle melted butter evenly over the top.

Cook on low for 3-4 hours.

20. Apple Barbecue Pulled Turkey Sandwiches

Ingredients
2 pounds turkey, shredded
2 apples, sliced
1 onion, chopped
1/2 cup applesauce
1 teaspoon chili powder
1 teaspoon cumin
1 cup barbecue sauce
1/2 cup chicken broth
1 garlic clove, minced
Pinch of salt and pepper
Sliced bread.

Instructions
In your slow cooker, bring together the turkey, onion and apples. In a bowl, mix the applesauce, chili powder, cumin, barbecue sauce, chicken broth, garlic, salt and pepper.

Pour the mixture over the turkey in your slow cooker. Cover and cook on low for 4 hours. Spoon the apple barbecue pulled turkey onto sandwich bread and serve warm.

21. Sweet Potato Turkey Shepherds Pie

Ingredients
3 cups sweet potatoes, mashed
1 pound turkey, shredded
2 cups peas
2 cups carrots
1/2 cup beef broth, or water
1 onion, chopped
2 cloves garlic.

Instructions
Reheat shredded turkey in a skillet, adding in the chopped onion and garlic. Bring this mixture to your slow cooker and add in the peas and carrots.

Pour the 1/2 cup of broth or water into your slow cooker and stir together. Spread the mashed sweet potatoes evenly over the top of the mixture.

Cover and cook on low for 5 to 6 hours. Then, remove the cover and turn to high for 30 minutes to crisp the sweet potato topping.

www.ingramcontent.com/pod-product-compliance
Lightning Source LLC
Chambersburg PA
CBHW072009070526
44583CB00015B/1396